CONTENT

CW01497363

Chapter 1
Introduction—What is Stitch & Tape Boat Construction?   **5**

Chapter 2
Tools, Skills & the Workshop   **9**
2.1   Tools   9
2.2   Skills   10
2.3   The Workshop   10

Chapter 3
Material for Stitch & Tape Construction   **11**
3.1   Wood   11
3.1.1 Plywood   11
3.1.2 Timber (Softwoods)   12
3.1.3 Timber (Hardwoods)   12
3.2   Glues & Fastenings   12
3.3   Developments in Epoxies   14
3.4   Possible Problems with Epoxies   14
3.4.1 The Epoxy Will Not Cure   14
3.4.2 Failure in the Bond of Components being Glued Together   15
3.4.3 Cloudy Appearance in Epoxy Coatings   15
3.4.4 Runs in the Epoxy Coating   15
3.4.5 Other Coating Products will not Cure over Epoxy   16

Chapter 4
Producing the Hull Planks   **17**
4.1   Marking Out the Hull Planks   17
4.2   Cutting Out the Hull Planks   20

Chapter 5
Joining Long Planks Together   **21**
5.1   General   21
5.1.1 Butt Straps   21
5.1.2 Scarf Joining Planks   24
5.1.3 Saw Tooth or Castellated Join   25

Chapter 6
Stitching the Planks Together   **27**
6.1   Preparing the Planks for Stitching   27
6.2   Stitching the Planks   28
6.3   Overcoming Problems with Plywood that will not Bend into Shape   31
6.4   What to do if a Plank Breaks   32
6.5   Stitching the Transom in Place   33
6.6   Final Tightening of the Stitches   33

Chapter 7
Checking the Shape of the Boat   **35**

Chapter 8
Stitch and Tape Seams & Epoxy Filleting Frames etc in Place   **37**
8.1   General   37
8.2   Stitch & Tape using Polyester Resin   38
8.3   Stitch & Tape using Epoxy Resin   40
8.3.1   For Small boats & Canoes   40
8.3.1.1   Omitting the Tapes on the Outside of the Chine Seams   42
8.3.1.2   Eliminating Tape Bumps on the Outside of the Chine Seam   43
8.3.2   For Larger Boats   44
8.3.3   Combination Seam Joints   46
8.3.4   Bonding Plywood Frames to the Hull   46
8.3.5   General Notes on Epoxy & Bonding with Epoxy   47

Chapter 9
Fitting Out the Hull   **49**
9.1   General   49
9.2   The Gunwales   49
9.2.1   The Inwales   49
9.2.1.1   Simple Solid Inwales   49
9.2.1.2   Open Pattern Inwales   52
9.2.2   The Outwales   53
9.3   Solid Quarter Knees & Breast Hook   53
9.4   Taking Shapes off the Boat & Fitting Thwarts   54
9.5   Centreboards & Daggerboards   56
9.5.1   The Case   56
9.5.2   The Centre/Daggerboard   57
9.5.3   Fitting Pivots   58
9.5.4   Combined Case & Frame   58
9.6   The Decking   59
9.6.1   The Deck Structure   59
9.6.2   The Deck   62
9.7   Coamings   63
9.8   Bottom Boards   64

Chapter 10
Buoyancy (Floatation)   **65**
10.1   General   65
10.2   Type of Buoyancy (Floatation)   66
10.3   Disposition of Floatation (Buoyancy)   66
10.4   How Much Buoyancy (Floatation) Do I Need?   68
10.5   A Note on Self Righting   68

Content

Chapter 11
Sheathing, Coatings & Finishes $\quad$ **71**
11.1 $\quad$ Sheathing $\quad$ 71
11.2 $\quad$ Coating with Epoxies $\quad$ 74
11.3 $\quad$ Paint Finishes on Bare Wood $\quad$ 75
11.3.1 Preparing the Boat Prior to Painting $\quad$ 75
11.3.2 Eliminating the Bumps Caused by Tapes on the Outside of the Hull $\quad$ 77
11.3.3 Striking the Waterline or Boottop $\quad$ 78
11.4 $\quad$ Safety $\quad$ 79

Chapter 12
Masts and Spars $\quad$ **81**
12.1 $\quad$ General Notes $\quad$ 81
12.2 $\quad$ Materials for Wood Masts & Spars $\quad$ 81
12.3 $\quad$ Solid Masts & Spars $\quad$ 82
12.4 $\quad$ Hollow Masts & Spars $\quad$ 86
12.4.1 Round Section Hollow Masts & Spars $\quad$ 86
12.4.2 Rectangular Section Hollow Masts & Spars $\quad$ 88

Chapter 13
Appendices $\quad$ **89**
13.1 $\quad$ Skegs & Keels $\quad$ 89
13.1.1 For Dinghies & Small Dayboats $\quad$ 89
13.1.2 For Medium Sized Dayboats 14'-18' $\quad$ 90
13.1.3 On Larger Dayboats up to 22' $\quad$ 90
13.2 $\quad$ Bilge Keels $\quad$ 91
13.3 $\quad$ Simple Plywood Rudders $\quad$ 91
13.4 $\quad$ Notes on Simple Joinery $\quad$ 92
13.4.1 Marking & Cutting a Simple Joint $\quad$ 92
13.4.2 Other Useful Joints $\quad$ 95
13.4.3 The Parts of a Simple Stitch & Tape Boat $\quad$ 96

On this page -three views of a 15' Northumbrian Coble being built by Sam Hotchins. Top photograph—all but the final plank stitched in place. Centre photograph—chine seams taped and frames epoxied in place and bottom photograph - being fitted out with framework for the seats and benches.

Chapter 1

INTRODUCTION

WHAT IS STITCH & TAPE BOAT CONSTRUCTION?

What often stops many people from building a boat is the cost, time or perhaps, a lack of confidence in their own abilities. The easiest, quickest and often, the most low cost way of building a boat is by using the stitch and tape method – in other countries it also goes by the name of 'tack and tape' or 'epoxy and tape' or stitch and glue. I wrote the Manual of Modern Small Plywood Boat Construction many years ago to largely cover this method, but time has moved on and whilst the basic techniques have not changed much, I thought it time to look at how a stitch and tape craft is fitted out, the spars are made and the whole project finished with some new examples – hence this new book. I also thought it a good idea to take a look at fitting flotation/buoyancy—how much buoyancy is required and where it should be placed.

So, what is the stitch and tape boat building method? - in a nutshell, this building technique simply takes pre-shaped hull planks/panels (from shapes given on the plans) and stitches them together along their mating edges to form a hull shell. To give the shell some rigidity and proper shape, a basic amount of framework in the form of plywood bulkheads and girders is often fitted into the hull shell and all the joins are then finished with epoxy and glass tape. The old method of building a plywood boat entailed making quite an extensive rigid framework first and then fitting the plywood over-size and trimming it to shape – hence the name 'ply on frame'. The 'ply on frame method' requires the use of some good woodworking skills and

Above—the planks have been stitched together in this example of a Selway Fisher Ptarmigan 17 Pocket Cruiser by Mr. P. Phillips—the rectangular pieces of plywood going across the planks are simple butt straps used to join the 8' (2.44m) lengths of plywood together.

many components which, after the hull has been planked, become effectively redundant or at least, over sized for their job. So, the old method worked from the inside-out (framework first, followed by planking) and the new stitch and tape method works from the outside-in (planking first, followed by less framework).

With modern materials, there is no need for you to be a craftsman or qualified boat builder or even an expert in DIY. This is not to say that if you have certain skills as a craftsman, you should not use them, but if you do make a mistake or do not achieve a close fitting joint, there is no need to worry, with modern epoxies.

The first reason for this, is that epoxy filleting will cover up inaccurate joints and if you follow some simple steps, the epoxy fillet itself can be made to look good. Secondly, with the way in which the epoxies work, it is often not a good idea to have a joint that is so tight that it leaves little room for the epoxy glue or fillet.

There must be a disadvantage of course, and initially this is in the cost of the epoxy resins. But the advantages they give to the stitch and tape building method namely, physical strength and their ability to speed up and simplify the building process, are well worth their expense.

Epoxy material costs can get out of hand in larger boats and it is not necessary to use them throughout the construction of your boat (although being able to say that your boat is entirely epoxy bonded and sealed can be a very good resale point) and this book will point out areas where money can be saved through the use of other more conventional glues and adhesives.

Polyester resins (as used in the majority of grp boat construction) are a good deal cheaper than epoxies and often more readily available, but are nowhere near as strong in tension or compression and they shrink by 5% of their volume when curing, which causes problems when using them for sheathing. However, they do have their place in ply stitch and tape construction and I often use both materials on the same boat, using epoxies in the high stress areas and polyesters elsewhere.

However, one reason why so many home boat building projects end up half complete, is because it is the fitting out of the boat that takes so much time and often far more time than it takes to make the hull. When I worked for D.M. Russell Marine (formerly Jas. A. Silver) we fitted out a grp Colvic/Watson 34'6'' hull as a large motor sailer with a wooden deck and superstructure. At Boat Shows we often used to get people on the boat who had just purchased a set of mouldings that they were going to fit out for themselves. When we told them that it took us 8000 professional man hours to fit the boat

Above—the same Ptarmigan 17 with planks stitched and taped together and the framework in place—note how little there is.

out, which represents 4 years work for 2 people working 20 spare time hours per week, they often withdrew in horror. Cutting out standard traditional wood fillets in the construction of furniture, bunks etc or in fitting bulkheads etc and replacing them with epoxy fillets, which can be moulded to any shape and which are put on with a spatula, will cut out many hours of work.

Also, if the designer has done his job properly, he will have used as many internal joinery components as possible as structural members, cutting out a lot of duplication in both materials and labour and greatly simplifying the internal framework of the boat.

The stitch and tape boats that come from the Selway Fisher drawing board are a blend of modern labour saving materials with pre-shaped dual purpose components which are put together in easy prefabricated structures . This allows you to do away with expensive and time consuming building moulds which later become redundant.

Whilst this book has been primarily set up to

complement the Selway Fisher catalogue of plans, the boat builder will find it a useful reference no matter who's plans or which kit, he is working from. Indeed, if he is working from a dated set of plans, which does not make use of modern epoxies and construction techniques then this manual will help him to make parts of his project more efficiently.

Above all, the boat building experience should be an enjoyable one and should not lead to having an unfinished millstone around your neck. The right combination of modern/traditional methods and materials used in the design and construction of your project, will greatly enhance your chances of completing a successful project and with this book, which is intended to be a handy reference for those who want to get onto the water quickly and at low cost, you will have a good chance of success.

Modern Computer Aided Design (CAD) facilities can go hand in hand with ply/epoxy or stitch and tape construction methods in helping the designer develop accurate hull plank and frame shapes. I have been asked to take older 'ply on frame' designs and model the hull on the CAD system so that it's hull plank shapes can be accurately developed for modern stitch and tape construction – the Yachting Monthly Senior and Heron dinghy are notable examples and so, with the right permissions, it is perfectly feasible to rejuvenate an old and classic design, making it more accessible to a new generation of boat owners. Do contact Selway Fisher if you have such a project in mind and we can then see how to use the method outlined in this book to produce a successful project.

Finally, let me say that the stitch and tape method is not an excuse to build a badly constructed boat—it is an excellent method for the home boat builder and especially for the first time builder but it is also a method often used by professional builders too and examples can be made to very high standards of finish—we will see if we can help you get close to such standards in your own efforts.

I do hope you enjoy this volume and find it a useful tool in getting you onto the water with the least amount of fuss and expense.

Paul Fisher
2009

Above—Mr. Phillip's beautifully built Ptarmigan 17, finished, launched and now just waiting for the wind.

Left—Sam Hotchin's 15' Northumbrian Coble performing well on a reach.

Chapter 2
TOOLS, SKILLS & THE WORKSHOP

2.1 Tools

Let us talk about a minimum tool kit to start with. We are not using thick plywood or large sections of timber and much of what is required can be bought pre-machined to the correct size from ordinary DIY stores and timber merchants Therefore there is no need for a large or extensive tool kit. My minimum kit includes :

For marking out:
- A 4' straight edge (or a good straight piece of timber).
- A 10' tape measure (or longer if possible).
- Several good sharp pencils (I keep loosing them!).
- A carpenter's square.
- A plumb line (can be a large nut or bolt attached to a piece of string).
- A carpenter's spirit level.

For cutting out and shaping:
- A domestic single speed jig saw.
- A small block plane.
- An 18mm chisel.
- A tenon saw (one of the cheap DIY variety will do).
- A 10 oz. (or heavier if you prefer) hammer.
- A nail punch.
- A screw driver to fit 8G size screws.
- An electric single speed drill or a hand drill with drill bits up to 6mm in dia.
- A Bradawl
- At least 8 off 4'' G clamps.
- A Black & Decker type Workmate folding bench.

Consumable Items—these are items other than tools, that you will need during the construction process:

- Large/small yogurt type pots - for glue/resin mixing.
- Mixing sticks - like large lollipop sticks.
- Barrier cream - to protect your hands.
- Acetone - for cleaning items coated in resin.
- Masking tape - for holding some items together whilst gluing and for masking off areas that you do not want covered in glue/resin.
- String/rope for use as tourniquets and Spanish windlasses to hold panels in place during the stitching process.

2.2 Skills

The skills required depend on the standard of finish you want to achieve. I always say that basic DIY home skills are all that are required for stitch and tape construction. These are the ability to measure onto wood using sizes etc on the plans, basic cutting with hand tools and drilling plus the ability to use a jig-saw without injuring yourself!

But, if you want to show off exposed wood joints then you will need some further skills of the kind learnt in Wood-Working or Design Technology lessons at school—remember the teapot stand and garden dibber you made? These projects used the simple cross halving join and the mortice and tenon—the former is useful for stitch and tape construction but the latter is not really necessary. But just to re-hone your skills go to the Appendices at the back of this book where you can re-learn the processes involved.

2.3 The Workshop

It is always good to have a large dry, well ventilated, well lit and well heated workshop. But not everyone has such a facility. I have used very cramped, damp and dark places which have so many holes in the walls that heating would be impossible—but you can get around these difficulties.

So what size of workshop do we need? The basic recommended minimum is for a floor area which is twice the plan area of your boat. In other words if your boat measures 20' (6m) in length by 8' (2.4m) in beam this represents a rectangular plan area of 160 square feet (14.4 sq.m.) and therefore your workshop should have no less than 320 square feet (28.8 sq.m.) in plan area This means that if you have a workshop with a length of 24' just 4' longer than the boat it's width should be no less than 13' which again represents only 5 feet more than the width of the boat or 2 1/2' on either side.

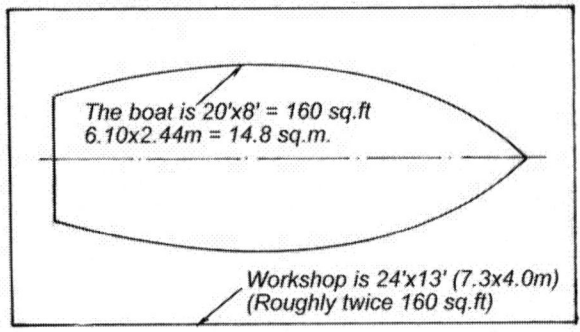

The boat is 20'x8' = 160 sq.ft
6.10x2.44m = 14.8 sq.m.

Workshop is 24'x13' (7.3x4.0m)
(Roughly twice 160 sq.ft)

Fig 1. Workshop size.

This does not really allow for much in the way of a bench and any machinery that you might have. You must also think about the height of the workshop. The height of an average garage/workshop may be around about 7' (2.1m)) but such a height can cause problems when you are trying to swing long pieces of timber around and will necessitate taking the timber out of the front of the workshop turning it around and walking back into the workshop with it again. If this is the case, then you must make sure that you have good turning room in front of the workshop.

Chapter 3

MATERIALS

FOR STITCH & TAPE CONSTRUCTION

3.1 Wood

3.1.1 Plywood

I have to say that I have met a lot of genuine Exterior grade WBP ply which is better than supposed Marine ply. True Marine ply will have veneers of equal thickness and of high quality (which usually means close grained). What often goes for Marine plywood, especially at 1/4'' (6mm) thickness, has a thick baulk core with very thin Gaboon outside veneers—Figure 2.

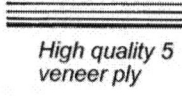

High quality 5
veneer ply

Lower quality 3 veneer ply with a
thick baulk core and wafer thin
outer veneers

Fig 2. Plywood quality.

The Gaboon plywood usually originates from the Far East and can certainly be used. It can come apart, with the veneers separating, if it is bent or stressed too much but this is rare. I find that it is no better than much of the baulk core 3 veneer Exterior ply. A good quality Marine ply at a reasonable cost is BS1088 Meranti Marine ply which still has a thick core veneer, but which has stronger outside veneers made of a durable timber.

Aquaply and similar high quality plywoods are a multi-laminate ply and are Lloyds/RNLI approved. They are excellent, though less easy to bend than Meranti or Gaboon ply and is expensive.

I have often used exterior WBP ply for dinghies and canoes with great success but do be careful of weaknesses caused by voids in the Core veneer. European or Israeli exterior is the best. Far Eastern WBP tends to have all sorts of defects, but I have used it without failure.

You must simply watch out for voids and make sure that they are not put under stress. I have been asked about the suitability of Fir ply, especially since it is used in some countries for hull construction. The trouble is, it comes in so many grades, from the lowest grade shuttering ply to a grade which probably matches reasonable WBP Exterior. This is often coated with epoxies to make the ply last longer. My own opinion is, that with the cost of the epoxy, you may as well use Meranti Marine ply and feel safer about the quality of the hull surrounding you.

3.1.2 Timber (Softwood)

Because of the cost, I often use 1st quality White Pine (Deal) rather than Douglas Fir or Spruce, with as few knots as possible. It tends to go black when it gets wet for any length of time but is easily worked and is quite strong. Be careful about coating over screw holes etc as this is where the wood often goes black. If you want higher quality Douglas Fir is a good compromise because it is relatively cheap and excellent for structural items. It is available in long lengths and is often used for solid spars. Western Red Cedar is an excellent lightweight wood. It is not as strong as Douglas Fir and it can also be expensive and is therefore only used for racing craft. Sitka

Spruce has a good strength to weight ratio and is used for long items such as stringers, spars etc. Cost is high.

3.1.3 Timber (Hardwood)

I do not intend going into all the suitable hardwoods because it is the policy of Selway Fisher Design to keep the costs of constructing our boats down to a minimum and therefore to exclude expensive hardwoods where ever possible. It is a good idea to use them where there is a high degree of stress for instance for mast steps, floors etc. or in areas subject to wear. So I shall simply mention a few that I have used and which are readily available.

Keruing is cheap and durable but very hard to work (especially to plane) and is very heavy. It suffers from resinous voids. Iroko (sometimes known as African Teak) is an excellent wood which is cheap and has many of the properties and the durability of Burma Teak. It can warp after cutting and is therefore better used in thinner sections and laminated together and should be well fastened down. Afromosia is very durable and is easy to work with and is available in large sizes.

Brazilian Mahogany is an excellent material but is expensive. As an alternative Khaya is less durable but cheaper and usually easier to work. White Oak is very good and has less tendency to warp in thinner sizes but may need washing down with an agent to get rid of it's natural oil, before being glued.

3.2 Glues & Fastenings

DO NOT use PVA or any glue which does not say that it is definitely waterproof (water resistant is not good enough). This may sound obvious, but mistakes have been made!

The cheapest marine glue in the larger quantities, was Cascamite (it also goes under the name Extramite), which is excellent for all general joiner work. However, it takes several hours to dry and is absolutely rigid and brittle and will therefore fracture if it is used to fill large gaps which are then stressed. Aerolite 306 I have found to be excellent and comes in 2 parts. It dries clear and will take a certain amount of flexing and is therefore good for varnished spars. Cascamite dries to a cream colour. Aerodux is also very good but difficult to buy in small quantities and dries to a dark brown colour.

Another glue which has come onto the market is Balcotan 100 which has the advantage of being a one component glue. It is a polyurethane glue which cures on contact with moisture. It is used straight out of the container with no preparation or modification and comes in two types, regular and rapid. Regular cures in 4 to 8 hours and Rapid cures in 15 to 60 minutes depending upon the temperature. It seems to have fewer possible allergy problems than the epoxies because unlike the epoxies, it does not contain solvents and gives off little in the way of vapours.

On curing, it expands slightly and will readily fill gaps. However, it should not be used to fill gaps due to poor fitting joints - as far as I am aware, it is not designated as a gap filling glue (ie., a glue which will fill a gap and still be stronger than the surrounding wood). Because it expands on curing, the components of the joint should be well fastened together either by mechanical fastenings (screws and nails etc) or cramps to resist the glue pushing the components apart. I have seen no real technical literature on it's strength in comparison to epoxies or other glues but, because of it's foaming/expanding properties, I can only assume that it will not

have the same shear strength as epoxy. However, where the wood joint has a large faying (surface) area, then, it's ease of use makes an ideal choice. I have used it successfully in the gluing up of laminated knees, general joinery inside a boat and for the gluing up of masts and spars.

Balcotan 100 has other advantages, not least being the fact that it does not need 'filling' with microfibres etc. It is already a glue, un-like the epoxies which are resins and which therefore need 'filling' before than can be used as glues. 'Filling' an epoxy resin means that it will go less far and partly because of this, you end up using less Balcotan 100 than you would epoxy. Indeed, although not confirmed, you may only use a third of the amount of epoxy that you would need to use, when using Balcotan. Typically, the strip planking of a 16' canoe may use 3kg of epoxy resin to glue the planks together, but only 1 kg of Balcotan 100.

Cleaning the joints up is also easier when using a polyurethane glue. With epoxy and most other glues, you must clean up the surrounding wood before any excess glue cures, trying to remove cured epoxy from around a joint often damages the wood. However, with Balcotan 100, you simply let any excess glue cure and then remove it with a cabinet scraper.

Most joints, if well glued, can be nailed rather than screwed, and I would recommend Gripfast barbed ring nails. Use the longest that the bury (total thickness of wood to be nailed) will allow. 12G are good for general use with 10G for heavy use. Brass boat nails can be used for low stress areas (ie., for nailing 1/4'' (6mm) ply seats onto supporting wood fillets). Because of their cost, I only use screws (brass or bronze) on joints which need to be pulled together or which are main structural (wood fillet cleats to frames, centreboard case etc.) and subject to high stress.

Nailing Schedule

Plywood Thickness	Nail Gauge	Nail Length	Staggered Spacing
1/4"/6mm	14G	7/8"/22mm	3"/75mm
3/8"/9mm	12G	1 1/4"/39mm	4"/100mm
1/2"/12mm	10G	1 1/2"/36mm	4"/100mm
5/8"/15mm	8G	2"/50mm	5"/125mm
3/4"/18mm	8G	2 1/4"/56mm	5"/125mm

3.3 Developments in Epoxies

The epoxies mentioned in Chapter 8 for work on stitch and tape joints are all of a general purpose type of which there are now several manufacturers and suppliers. Over the past few years some manufacturers have been developing new epoxies to suit particular applications. For instance, whilst the general purpose resins can be difficult to use when applying woven cloth because of their relatively high viscosity, some have developed lower viscosity resins for use with woven fabrics but which can also be filled to produce a filleting material. For instance Structural Polymers have their SP320 Spacote which has been developed as a lower viscosity resin for use with woven fabrics but which can also be filled to produce a filling material. Structural Polymers have also produced SPll0/210 specifically for woven fibre laminating and SP Spabond purely as a bonding adhesive—there are various derivatives for different applications including Spabond370 which is specifically for gluing Teak..

There is no doubt that these materials offer physical advantages over the simple use of a general purpose resin as a multi purpose material for gluing/bonding, filleting and the application of glass tape, but in using specialist materials you will inevitably end up spending more on small boat construction where you may end up with a whole load of half used products. It is very difficult to estimate the quantities of epoxies etc., required on a particular job as I have known some builders use half the epoxy on a particular boat, that somebody else uses on the same boat. However, for larger jobs and especially where you intend to coat an entire boat in epoxy, these new systems will provide an easier and better finished job.

3.4 Possible Problems with Epoxies

3.4.1 The Epoxy Will Not Cure

If the epoxy does not fully cure in the recommended time, there are several possible simple reasons. The first area to check, is that the correct mixing ratio has been used. In low temperatures, allow extra curing time and gently apply more localised heat (perhaps by building a temporary PVC shelter over the area being epoxied and using a low power heater).

Insufficient mixing can also be a problem, which is why I prefer to mix up small amounts of resin and hardener. The smaller amount being mixed, the easier it is to ensure a thorough mixing of resin and hardener.

Remember that it is essential to mix the resin and hardener together before mixing any fillers and additives to the mix.

3.4.2 Failure in the Bond of Components being Glued Together

If we assume that the epoxy/filler mix has fully cured, then bond failure is most often due to a resin starved glue join. This can occur for two reasons. Either the porosity of the wood has caused the resin in the glue mix to 'soak' away from the joint or, too much clamping pressure has been applied and the epoxy mix has been squeezed out from the join.

If the wood is very porous or if you are gluing together end grain wood then 'prime' the wood first with unfilled resin/hardener. End grain should be 'primer' coated and the resin allowed to cure before further resin/hardener is applied and then before this coat cures, the thickened bonding resin is also applied and the join put together.

Also make sure that the surfaces to be bonded are not contaminated and that the bonding area is sufficiently large for the purpose of the joint.

3.4.3 Cloudy Appearance in Epoxy Coatings

Cloudy/white areas seen in the coating after the resin has cured are most often caused by moisture either from condensation or from very humid conditions. Coating early in the morning is usually a bad idea. Do any epoxy coating mid day or in the afternoon. If you have sanded down the previous resin coat using wet and dry sand paper do make sure that there is no moisture left on the surface before applying the next epoxy coat.

The only way to get rid of this cloudiness, is to cut the resin coats back by sanding down and then to wash the surface down to remove the amine blush. Make sure that all surfaces are thoroughly dry and then re-coat.

Cloudiness can also be caused by over vigorous brushing or rolling on of the epoxy coat. This traps air in the resin which does not escape and again this will have to be cut back to remove the cloudiness. You should also use a special coating resin or one which uses a different hardner to make the epopxy less viscous (WEST 207 special coating hardener for instance). As with painting and varnishing, always apply resin coats in thin layers.

3.4.4 Runs in the Epoxy Coating

This is caused by too thick a coat of resin being applied or perhaps the resin taking too long to cure. So the cure is either to warm the resin before applying it or too use a faster hardener. Overall, I have found that simply putting the resin container into a bowl of hot water to raise it's temperature is the best solution. Not only does this raise the temperature of the resin so that it cures quicker after application but it also lowers the viscosity of the resin so that it is easier to apply and also goes further too. In fact, when I am using the epoxy to wet out glass tape for stitch and tape seams, I always pre-heat the resin container in warm water and I find that the resin wets out the glass tape easier allowing you to use less resin. This is an important tip when taping in cool temperatures. I have been able to halve the amount of resin used by pre-heating as against trying to use it in it's cold state.

3.4.5 Other Coating Products will not Cure over Epoxy

In this case, the epoxy may not have fully cured. I always leave epoxy coatings three to four days or more in temperatures of at least 60 degrees before over coating with paint or varnish.

There may also be a problem with compatibility between the hardener used in the epoxy and the coating being used. Single part polyurethanes may not cure over epoxy. In the main. I have found little trouble with most conventional oil based paints (for instance many exterior household paints) but they do sometimes take more time to cure. If possible, do a test piece before committing yourself to a particular paint or varnish system.

Preparation of the epoxy surface before applying the paint or varnish is essential. Make sure that any amine blush is removed and that the surface is well sanded before applying the coating—see 3.4.4.

If a paint or varnish is not curing after it has been applied over an epoxy coated surface, I leave it to dry as far as possible over a day or two and then wash it down with white spirit. I then allow this to dry and coat with another thin coat of paint or varnish—usually this works.

Chapter 4
PRODUCING THE HULL PLANKS

4.1 Marking Out the Planks

The first stage of building a stitch and tape boat is to mark and cut out the plywood planks. Plank shapes are rarely successful when given full-size unless they are plotted onto expensive Mylar sheets – plotting onto ordinary paper is not very accurate as the paper will shrink and stretch and for larger boats with long panels/planks, this can be disastrous. Over the years I have had several clients talk to me about the problems that they have encountered using full-size templates mainly due to slight variations in the plotting scale which should of course be full-size or 1:1 but is not always so and a small discrepancy can be disastrous over an 8' (2.44m) length of plank.

On Selway Fisher Design plans we use a simple method of accurately marking out the plank/panel shapes directly onto the plywood sheets. It does involve the use of a tape measure and transferring measurements given on the drawings onto the sheets of plywood, but it is accurate. Alternatively, you can go to one of the growing firms who can take our DXF files and use them to router or laser cut the panels for you (www.jordanboats.co.uk for instance). To mark out the planks/panels yourself, follow this simple method :-

A.   Look at the design sheet showing the hull panel/plank shapes and you will see a drawing showing one or more standard sheets of plywood laid edge to edge with the panel/plank shapes drawn on them and a series of parallel station lines drawn across the ply. These are usually spaced at 305mm (12") intervals. The dimensions for the panel/plank shapes are measured along these station lines – so the first job is to draw these

17

station lines down onto the plywood – see
Figure 3.

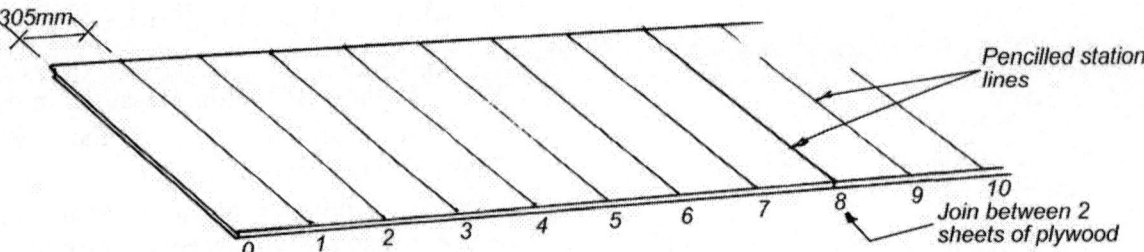

Fig 3.

B.   Next, put your tape measure along each
of these station lines in turn and mark off the
dimensions given for the top and bottom
(chine, gunwale lines etc) of each panel –
Figure 4. Take your time and make sure you
make a bold mark for each measurement –
note that in most cases all the dimensions
given are measured from the lower edge of
the ply sheet.

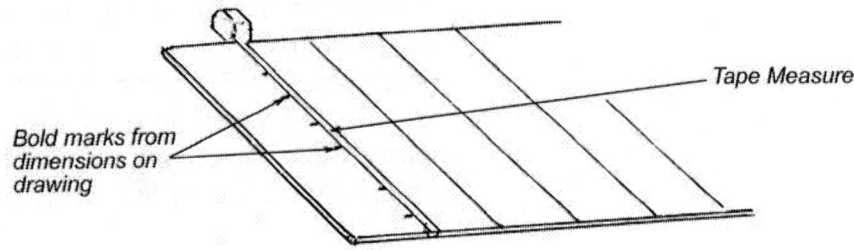

Fig 4.

C.   You can now mark the end points for
each line – for instance, at the bow end of
each panel the end points are defined by a
distance up from the lower edge of the
plywood sheet and horizontally from an
adjacent station line – see Figure 5.

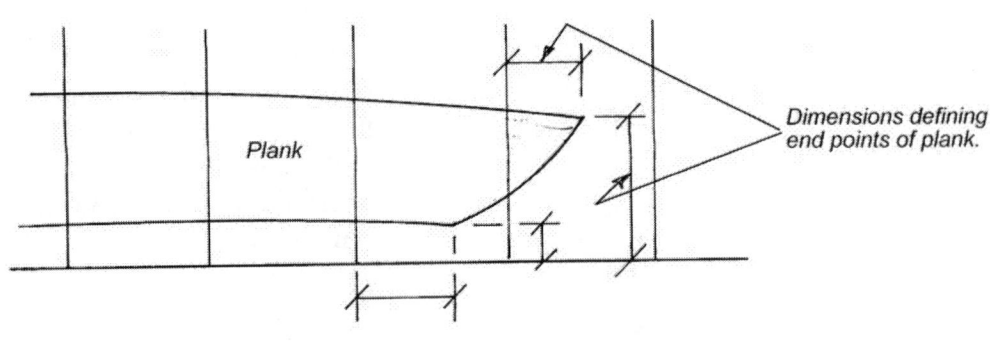

Fig 5.

D.   Sometimes a particular curve (often a bow end curve), is defined by a series of squares – see Figure 6 – the size of the squares will be given – draw these onto the plywood sheet aligned as shown against a station line, and sketch in the curve using the squares as a guide.

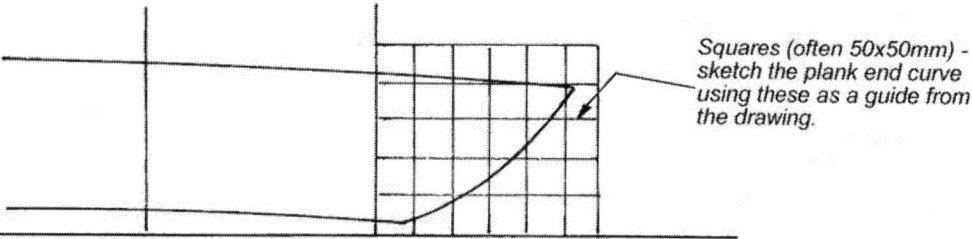

Squares (often 50x50mm) - sketch the plank end curve using these as a guide from the drawing.

Fig 6.

E.   Now we can draw in the long curves defining the panels/planks – do this using a long thin batten (a piece of old plastic curtain rail or thin plastic wiring conduit which you can obtain from a DIY store, is excellent for this) – hold the batten down with weights or nails to pass through each mark on the station lines and draw in each curve with a bold pencil line – see Figure 7.

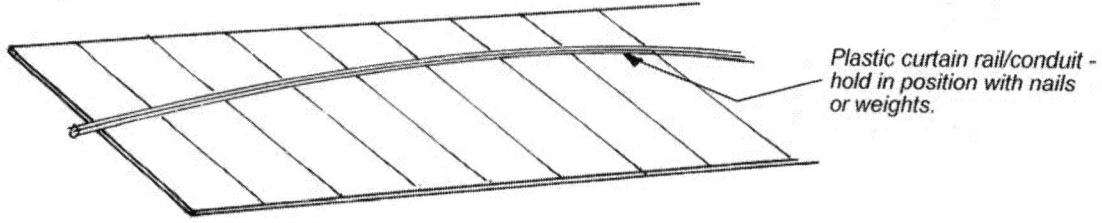

Plastic curtain rail/conduit - hold in position with nails or weights.

Fig 7.

F.   Mark any frame positions given on the drawings onto the hull panels/planks.

4.2 Cutting Out the Hull Planks

Now you can cut out the panel/plank shapes – I use a single speed jig saw with a fine blade holding the ply sheet on a workmate/saw horse – cut approximately 1mm from the line. You can either mark out each panel separately (port and starboard) or mark and cut out one set of panels (say the port side) and use these as templates for the other set (starboard side).

Some builders have successfully cramped (or bolted) 2 sheets of plywood together, one on top of the other and then used a jig-saw to cut the planks out of both sheets at one time. This means that there is only a need to mark out one set of planks. If you do this, use a new high quality jig-saw blade and make sure that the jig-saw foot is set accurately at 90 degrees to the blade and that the blade does not bend during the cutting so that the bottom plywood plank ends up smaller than the top plywood plank.

I have also hand cut planks using a Tenon saw held at a shallow angle, especially if there are no tight curves on the plank shapes. This takes a lot of effort but allows you to cut closer to the line and low grade plywood is less likely to shatter using a hand saw.

Once all the planks/panels have been cut out, you can use your workmate (bench vice etc) to hold each individual pair of panels together so that they can be planed up carefully to the line.

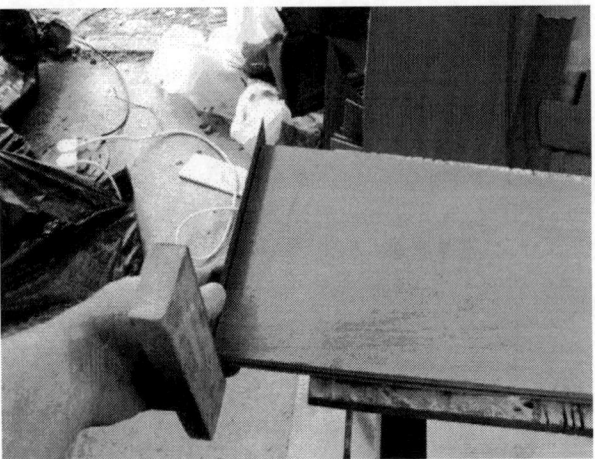

Match each pair of planks together and clamp each end.

Use a couple of workmates to hold the planks vertically and use a plane to trim them down to the line.

A square is used to make sure that you are planning/trimming the edges all the same and not taking too much off one side or the other.

5.1 General

For any boat over 7'9" long, the plank lengths will need to be joined at some point when using standard 8' (2.44m) sheets of plywood. There are 2 basic/common methods of joining ply planks together which are longer than the standard 8' (2440 mm) sheets of ply. These are the Butt Strap and Scarf methods.

The Butt strap is the simplest method and is strong but does leave a rather ugly block on the inside of the hull and can give you a hard spot on the hull. The Scarf joint is stronger (if it is done correctly) and is far neater and almost gives you a plank that looks continuous without any hard spots but it requires a long bench to work on and some careful use of the plane.

5.1.1 Butt Straps

For thin ply up to 4mm in thickness and for lightweight boats such as canoes, you can butt the ply together and simply tape the butt join both sides of the plank, with 3'' woven roving tape. This is the method employed on the Dart, Waterman and Wren canoes and is quick and simple (Figure 8). Apply the tape in the same way as mentioned in Chapter 8 priming the ply first with the resin. I have successfully used this method with polyester type 'A' resin but epoxy would of course, be stronger. Make sure that the ply planks are

3" (75mm) Woven Roving tape
both sides of butt join

Fig 8. A simple glass tape butt join.

Above—two parts of a plank butted together over softwood which has been covered in PVC and temporarily nailed in place (outside the glass butt strap area. The plywood has been given a coat of the epoxy resin/hardener mix ready for the tape to be applied.

Above—the glass tape has been applied and has thoroughly wetted out. This is now left to cure, the nails removed and the plank is carefully turned over ready to have a second glass tape applied on the other face of the plank.

held down onto a flat surface. It is better to do this with weights set either side of the join—or nail each piece down to a piece of softwood.

Boats made from 5 or 6mm ply and above, require ply butt straps. These are applied to the inboard side of the planks only and are of equal thickness to the ply plank. If the butt strap is not wide enough, then you will end

up with a hard spot where the ply plank moves away from lying in a flush line with it's mating part (Figure 9). On the other hand, if the strap is too wide, it will prevent the plank from bending around any curve that you have to induce into it when fitting it to the hull.

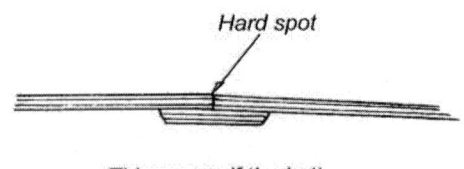

Hard spot

This occurs if the butt strap is not wide enough

Fig 9. A hard spot on the butt join.

I have found that 4" to 5" (100-125mm) wide butt straps are ideal for boats made from 1/4" (6mm) ply and 6" (150mm) for 3/8" (9mm) ply and 8" (200mm) for 1/2" (12mm) ply. The ply pieces of plank should be butt joined on a hard flat surface covered with pvc (to prevent any excess glue from attaching the ply to the work surface) and plenty of glue should be used during the process applying it to the mating edges of the pieces of ply plank first (Figure 10).

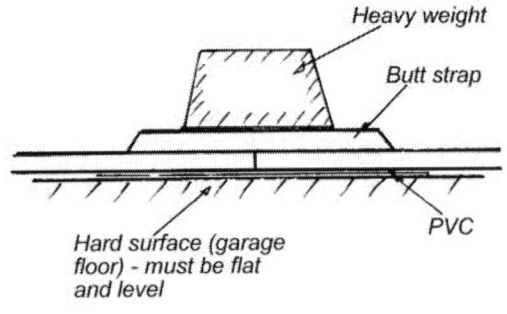

Heavy weight

Butt strap

Hard surface (garage floor) - must be flat and level

PVC

Fig 10. Applying a ply butt strap.

For piece of mind, I like to fasten the butt strap into place with boat nails. I do this by assembling one of the pieces of ply plank to the strap with the strap underneath and hammering the nails through from the outside so that they pass into a scrap piece of wood held under the strap (Figure 11). Apply more glue and fit the other piece of plank, and nail it in the same way. Carefully turn the plank over (you will need some help) and with a chisel remove the scrap pieces of wood exposing the ends of the nails. Having made sure that the planks are lying flat, you can then hammer the ends of the nails over to lie across the grain of the ply.

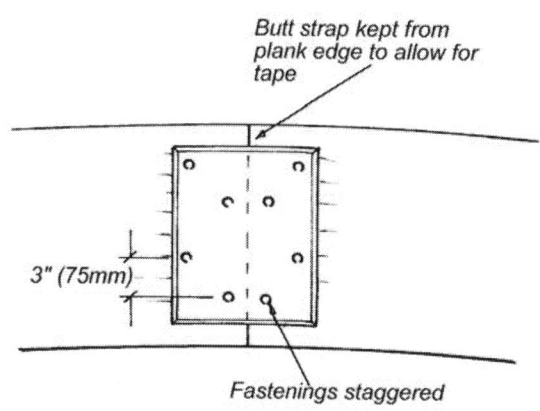

Fig 12. Larger butt straps.

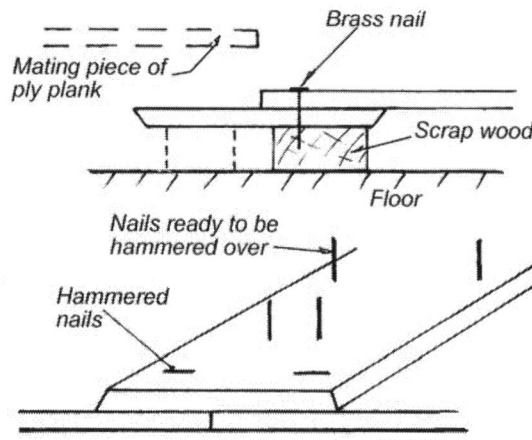

Fig 11. Nailing a butt strap—alternatively, use small screws.

If the plans you are working from do not specify the position of the butt straps in planks (some may also be needed for bulkheads etc) then position them away from frames and bulkheads and in such a manner, that straps on adjacent planks are not near each other. Also, take into account the inside WR tape on stitch and tape boats and cut the strap short to keep it clear of the edge of the ply so that the tape does not have to run over the strap.

For 3/8'' (9mm) ply and above, use screws instead of nails to fasten the straps. Both nails and screws should be put in staggered and at 3'' (75mm) spacing (Figure 12).

Above—a typical plywood butt strap on the planks of a 10'6" Northumbrian Coble and below, one set of planks with butt straps fitted and ready to start stitching the hull together—remember that the planks must be 'handed' with the butt straps on the inboard faces of the planks only.

5.1.2 Scarf Joining Planks

The length of a scarf joint should be 6 to 8 times the thickness of the plank, so that for a 1/4'' (6mm) plank, it should be around 2'' (50mm) long (Figure 13). Because you are not simply butting the planks together scarfing the planks will mean that you will have to allow for the length of the scarf when marking and cutting out the plank pieces. The best way to do this, is to mark out one part of the plank as normal, but then to start marking the mating piece of plank the length of the scarf joint away from the edge of the ply sheet. The lines for the edge of the plank should be projected back over the scarf allowance (Figure 14).

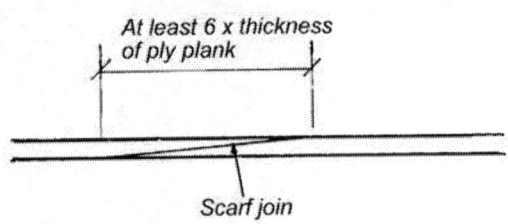

Fig 13. An edge-on view of a scarf join.

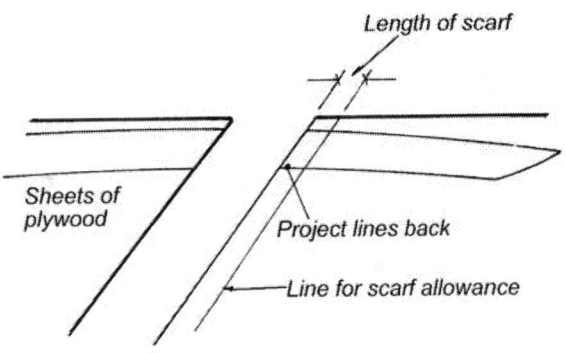

Fig 14. Marking out the planks with the additional width required for the scarf.

The best way to plane scarfs, is to do 2 or more at a time by clamping them to a bench top with the edge of the lower plank up to the edge of the bench and the next plank on top

of the first, but with it's edge butting up to the inner scarf line of the lower plank (Figure 15). Plane carefully with a sharp, finely set plane, using the plywood laminates as a guide. These will show as straight lines across the ply, if the surface that you are planing is flat. Check that the surface is good and flat with a straight edge.

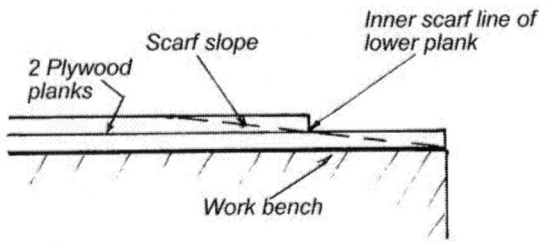

Fig 15. Setting up the planks.

Above—planning a scarf on two planks at once and using the plywood laminates as a guide.

When gluing the scarf joint, put pvc down first, apply the glue liberally and use heavy staples to hold the ply together and to prevent it from slipping whilst you clamp it up. This is a slightly delicate operation and it is best to have some patient help around. The cramps should be applied over lengths of wood above and below the joint so that the clamping pressure is spread evenly across the width of the joint. Use PVC (plastic shopping bags) between the lengths of wood and the plank to prevent them from sticking to the plank.

Above—clamping a scarf join.

Once the glue has cured, the cramps can be removed and the edges of the plank planed up. For scarfed planks especially, you may need to check that the planks have been correctly aligned (do this before the glue has cured!) by running a line between the lower fore and aft points of the plank and checking the measurement from the line to the middle lower edge of the plank against the drawings (Figure 16).

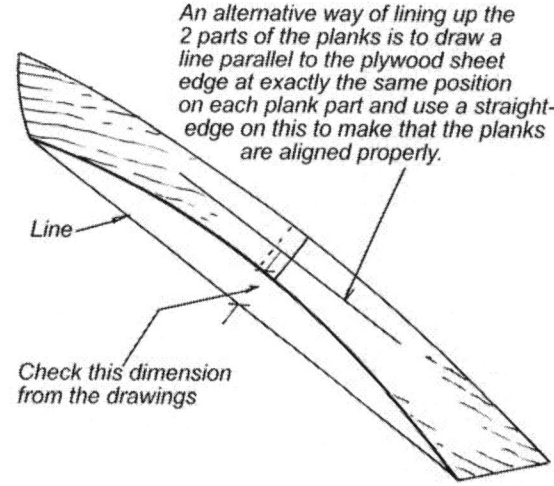

An alternative way of lining up the 2 parts of the planks is to draw a line parallel to the plywood sheet edge at exactly the same position on each plank part and use a straight-edge on this to make that the planks are aligned properly.

Line

Check this dimension from the drawings

Fig 16. Checking the overall shape of the plank.

5.1.3 Saw Tooth or Castellated Join

This is a rare but quite a neat and simple method of joining plank lengths together. Basically, a truncated saw tooth shape is cut into the end of one plank piece and it's matching shape is cut into the end of the other plank.

Figure 17 gives typical dimensions for a 120mm wide 6mm ply plank on the Selway Fisher Beach Punt 'Able'. This method is really appropriate for fairly narrow planks.

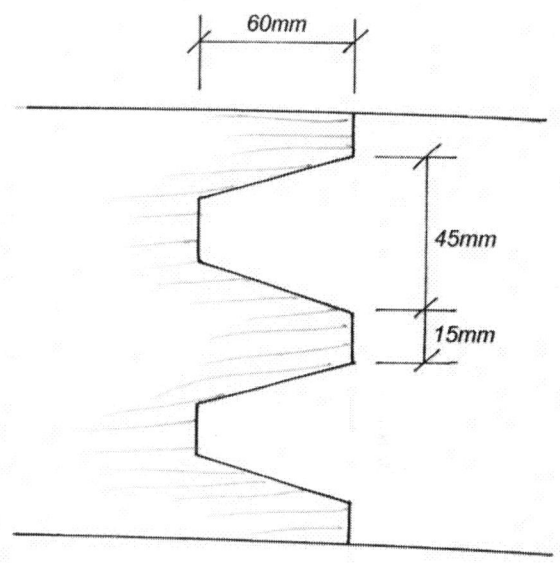

60mm

45mm

15mm

Fig 17. The shape of the saw tooth/castellated join in 6mm plywood.

First, carefully mark out the shape of the castellation onto the end of one plank/panel. Cut this out using a tenon saw to cut the lines that go along the plank (at an angle) and cut along the lines across the plank with a coping saw (I prefer to fully imprint these latter lines by using a chisel and mallet on them).

When marking out the plank shape onto the mating piece of ply, you must allow for the length of the join (in much the same way as you do for a scarf join) by adding this measurement onto the end of the plank. At this point, the plank piece which has already been cut out should be placed over the unmarked end of the second plank piece. Line up the two plank pieces very carefully, making sure that both pieces are positioned to give the correct plank curve and then clamp them together to prevent any movement.

Take a sharp pencil and using the plank already cut as a template, mark the shape onto the second piece of planking. This may then be carefully cut out.

Because the glue will be applied to end grain plywood, the end of the ply should be pre-coated with epoxy resin (allowing this to cure). Further thickened epoxy can then be applied and the two pieces of plank brought together. Lay the gluing pieces together onto a flat surface which has been covered with PVC and hold down with weights.

This is also a good method to use, if you intend joining oversize pieces of ply together before marking and cutting out the final plank shape.

Above—a saw tooth/castellated join in the planking of an Able Beach Punt by Ian Gardner.

Left—sometimes the length of a boat means that short pieces of ply need to be joined—as can be seen on this Electric Skiff built by Mr. D Brooks. This can be awkward, but, with modern glues producing joints which are stronger than the surrounding wood, the position of the joins along the length of the boat, is not so critical. Having joins in several planks in-line with each other, does not usually cause problems when using modern glues.

Chapter 6

STITCHING THE PLANKS TOGETHER

6.1 Preparing the Planks for Stitching

The planks now need to be stitched together along what are called the 'chine' seams—a 'chine' is simply the 'corner' between two planks on a plywood boat. So, the first job is to drill as many of the holes as you can to take the stitches. Precise measurement for the holes is not required as most of the stitches will be removed later and their spacing will not usually show up on the finished boat. The stitches may be copper wire (1/16'' in dia (1.5mm), for small dinghies to 1/8'' dia (3mm) for 18' (5.5m) boats with 3/8'' (9mm) ply hull panels) from scrap electrical cabling, iron binding wire (very cheap), gardening wire (nylon coated) and bailing wire, can be used. The main requirement is that it is strong enough to hold the joint together and ductile enough to be easily twisted together to form the tie.

Cable ties may also be used but I still prefer to use wire as once tightened, you cannot release cable ties and they can be expensive.

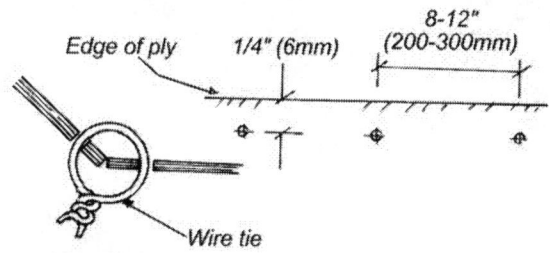

Fig 18. Drilling the holes for the stitches.

For 1/4" (6mm) ply, keep your drill holes about 1/4" (6mm) from the edge of the ply and unless the area is highly stressed the spacing between the ties can be between 8 and 12 inches (200-300mm) - Figure 18. Put in more ties where the shape requires it.

You cannot drill all the holes required as it is difficult to match holes in adjacent planks before you start to stitch. The rule is, at each chine seam, drill the holes in one plank only and then drill it's matching hole in the adjacent plank as you start to stitch the planks together and bend them into place. The only seam where this does not apply is the centreline seam on the first set of planks.

So, starting with the bottom pair of planks, lay them on a bench, match them up and drill the holes through both planks for the centreline seam. At the same time, drill the holes along the top of the planks for the first chine seam. Put this first pair of plank to one side and then repeat the process on the top edge of the remaining planks with the exception of the top most plank which you do not drill at all for the moment.

Above—drilling the first set of holes—do this over a bench or, if not convenient, hold a wood block under the planks as you drill so that the veneer on the underside plank does not break out as you drill through—be careful not to drill your hand!

6.2 Stitching the Planks

I am often asked whether to stitch the plywood frames in place at the same time as you stitch the planks together. It depends on the design and how stiff and awkward the planks are to get into place. I often find it a good idea to start stitching the frames into place after the first 2 or 3 planks have been loosely stitched together. You do not want everything to be too rigid at an early stage as there is often some adjustment, perhaps with a plane, to be made, especially towards the bows.

Lay the first pair of planks together and loosely stitch through the centre line seam but do not go too far up the curve of the bow. Now, whilst supporting the planks on a couple of work benches or saw horses, open them out—do not worry about getting the planks into their correct position at this stage.

Start stitching the next pair of planks in place using a reference point to start from—in a canoe this may be the centre seam where the plank lengths are joined together—in a dinghy it may be at a centre frame position. Keep the stitches loose so that adjustments fore and aft can be made later.

Just how far you start to pull the bow together at this stage, is a matter for careful consideration. Some samples of plywood are definitely much more stiff than others of the same thickness and manufacture. I also find that it is sometimes best to leave the bow entirely until I have all the planks stitched together—adjacent planks often help each other in forming the correct shape at the bow.

When you are stitching the bow there will be a lot of stress in bending the planks into place. In this area force the ply into the shape required for the edges of the panel to lie

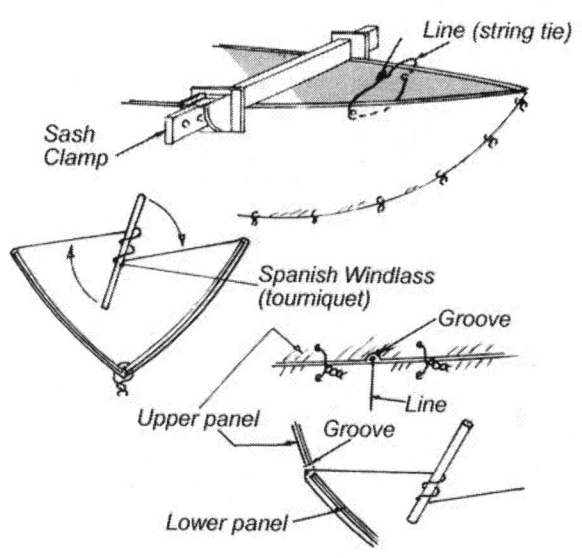

Fig 19. Using clamps and tourniquets to help force the planks into position.

Above—the second pair of planks has been attached to the first pair for most of their length on this 10'6" Northumbrian Coble—the first pair is temporarily closed at the bow by a cramp and the frames have been stitched into place.

together correctly, by using string ties. Whilst the ties are being secured, the ply can also be forced together with sash clamps and/or by using a Spanish Windlass on the tie (Figure 19). The string ties are passed through holes in the ply which will eventually be filled after the string has been removed. When the next panel of ply is stitched into place, the string can be accommodated in a small groove filed into the bottom edge of the next panel.

Right—two Spanish Windlasses used on the first planks of a 10'6" Northumbrian Coble getting them into position ready to accept the second pair of planks which have already been stitched in place for part of their length.

Above—a Spanish Windlass used on the planks of a 12' Fisher Swampscott Dory as they meet it's tombstone transom.

Above—you can see where three Spanish Windlasses have been used on the 10'6" Northumbrian Coble—two for the first plank and one for the second plank—these will be kept in position until the bow seam has been epoxied.

I repeat, whilst stitching the hull together, do not twist the wire too tight in case any adjustments need to be made. If there are any tight spots, release the wire and carefully trim the edges of the ply with a block plane (Figure 20).

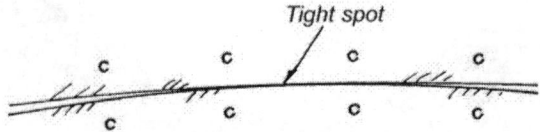

Fig 20. A 'tight' area along the chine seam.

Above—the stitches have been released in an area where one plank is too tight against another and a small block plane is being used to remove some material from the lower plank.

If you are stitching together a thicker ply then drill the holes for the wire ties further from the edge of the ply (3/8'' (9mm) away from the edge for 3/8'' (9mm) ply, 1/2'' (12mm) away for 1/2'' (12mm) ply).

If the ply is difficult to force into shape, steam it by wrapping the ply above and below in towels and pour boiling water over it. The towels will retain the water and heat and help the outer veneers (where there will be most tension and compression) to stretch and contract more easily (Figure 21). Initially soak the outside of the bend only as this may be all that is required, but if this does not succeed, soak both sides.

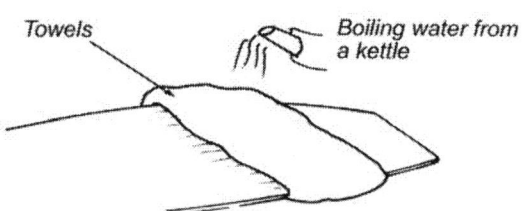

Fig 21. Using hot water to 'steam' a ply panel and make it more supple.

Plywood of the same thickness and specification but from different manufacturers will bend by different amounts. Good quality Marine ply with thin veneers (ie. 5 veneers in 1/4'' (6mm) ply) is much stiffer than lower quality ply which if it is of 1/4'' (6mm) thickness, may have just 3 veneers, the outside ones being very thin with a thick baulk core veneer (Figure 2).

6.3 Overcoming Problems with Plywood that will not Bend into Shape

Where there is difficulty in getting the ply to bend to the desired curve there are 2 alternatives that I have used.

The first, is to made up the thickness of ply in 2 layers (so that a 1/2'' (12mm) bottom can be made up out of 2 thicknesses of 1/4'' (6mm)). The problem here is to get the outside layer to adhere to the inside layer without voids and gaps between the 2 layers as the outside layer never bends in exactly the same way as the inside layer.

The best way to overcome this, is to put the outside layer on in diagonal strips say 4 to 6'' (100-150mm) wide which can be more easily held together (Figure 22). Gaps between the strips can be filled with epoxy but in any case

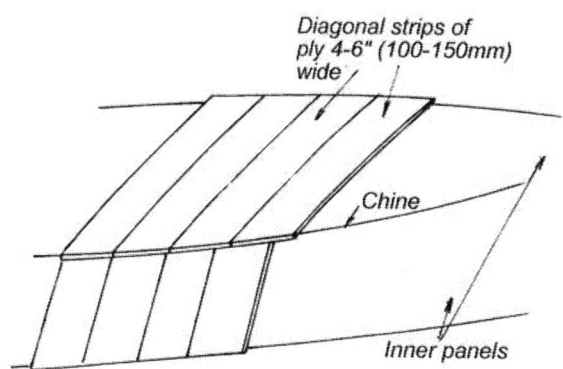

Fig 22. Using half thickness diagonal strips of ply over an area that will not allow a full thickness of ply to bend properly.

marking the shape of adjacent strips in heavily curved areas is not difficult (simply lay the new strip at say 1'' (25mm) distance from the last strip to be glued on and using a small block and pencil, scribe the shape with the block riding along the edge of the last strip) (Figure 23).

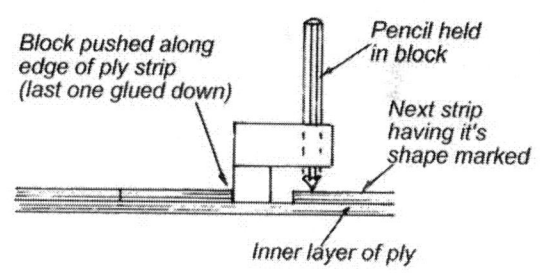

Fig 23. Marking the diagonal strips of plywood.

Large flat areas can be made up from the full thickness of ply with 4'' (100mm) of the edge of the ply cut back to accommodate the strips where they meet (Figure 24). To hold the ply layers together whilst the glue dries, use industrial staples. A hand operated machine is quite cheap and can be purchased

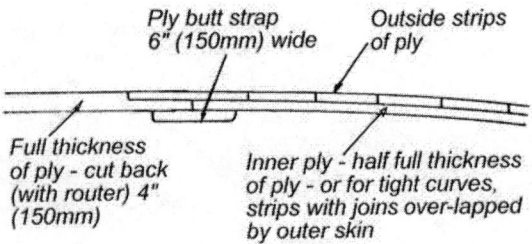

Fig 24. Applying the ply strips and marrying them to the full thickness ply.

from most DIY warehouses. The staples are inserted over lengths of tough cord which can be pulled up when the glue has dried so pulling the staples up and helping to remove them (Figure 25). Use plenty of glue in the process.

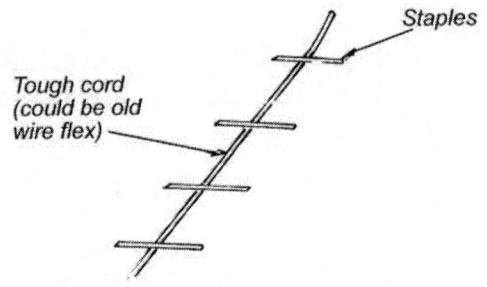

Fig 25. Stapling the outer strips to the inner skin.

The second method is to use the full thickness of ply but before it is applied use a circular saw with the blade set to half the thickness of the ply, to cut grooves across the inside face of the ply. These grooves should run perpendicular to the bend and be around 1/4'' (6mm) apart (Figure 26). Once the ply has been bent into place and the chine seams have been finished, the grooves are filled with epoxy and the inside face of the ply is covered in a layer of 8 oz. (280 gr.) woven roving (WR).

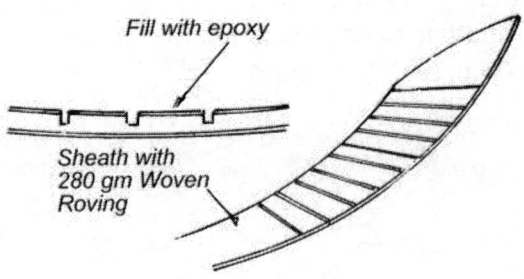

Fig 26. Saw cuts used to make the plywood more flexible.

Of the two methods, the first is certainly the stronger and neater although it takes more time.

6.4 What to do if a Plank Breaks

The first thing to do is not to panic. A plank breaking is tiresome but the problem can be overcome. First, check the break, it may be that you were unlucky enough not to notice a void going through the inner veneers of the plywood. In this case mark and cut out another plank on a good piece of plywood.

If the plywood was good but still broke you will need to consider one of the methods outlined in 6.3 but, in rare cases, there is sometimes a need, especially on designs where there is a lot of twist in the forefoot and the plank is wide, to revert back to a small portion of 'ply plank on frame construction'. You may have to put in some frame work to give yourself something to work too and this can be done with some partial stringers and an inner stem (Figure 27).

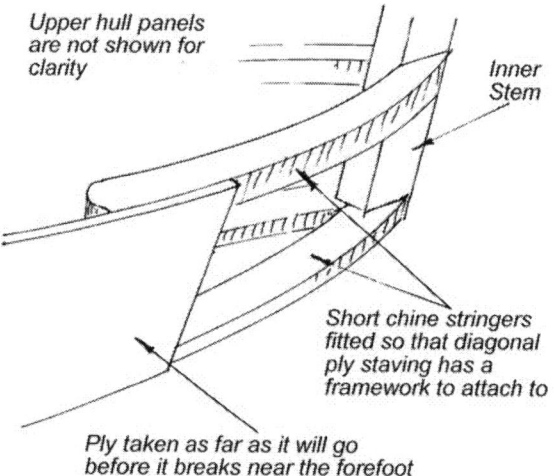

Upper hull panels are not shown for clarity

Inner Stem

Short chine stringers fitted so that diagonal ply staving has a framework to attach to

Ply taken as far as it will go before it breaks near the forefoot

Fig 27. Putting in partial framework to take conventional ply planking.

6.5 Stitching the Transom in Place

You can leave this until all the planks have been stitched or do it as you go. I tend to put it in after I have the first 2 or 3 pairs of planks together. The transom usually sits inside the planks so you want to drill a hole towards the top and bottom of each plank just ahead of the transom. Drill matching holes in the transom starting from the bottom and stitching before you drill the next hole.

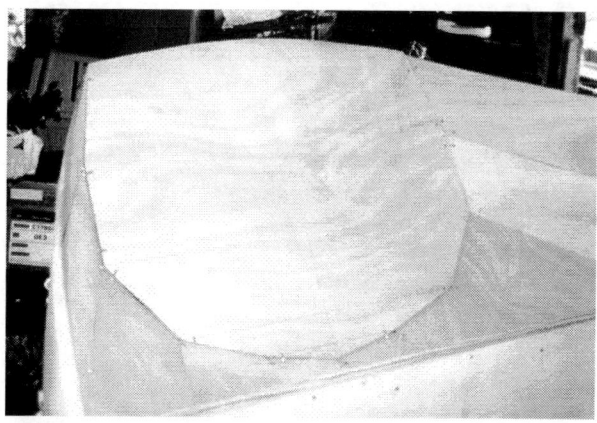

Above—the transom of a 10'6" Northumbrian Coble stitched in place—if a plank tends to bow away from the transom in it's centre, simply put another stitch in to hold it correctly in place.

6.6 Final Tightening of the Stitches

Once all the planks are in place along with the transom and frames, you can start to tighten all the stitches. Start at the centreline seam and work you way up each plank in turn—work from the middle towards the ends. As you do so push the planks so that the inner corners of the plank edges meet together and do not overlap.

Where two planks seem too tight together with gaps either side of the tight spot, release the wires so that you can use a small block plane to take of some material.

Gaps up to 3 or 4mm are no problem—anything more will need filling with a sliver of wood epoxied in place. Smaller gaps are dealt with by fixing a piece of masking tape to the outside of the seam and applying thickened epoxy to the gap on the inside of the chine seam. This is done when we start to prepare the seams for taping but not now because we have got to check the shape of the boat before going any further.

Above—a 3 or 4mm gap between the planks is left to be filled with thickened epoxy just before we start to tape the seams.

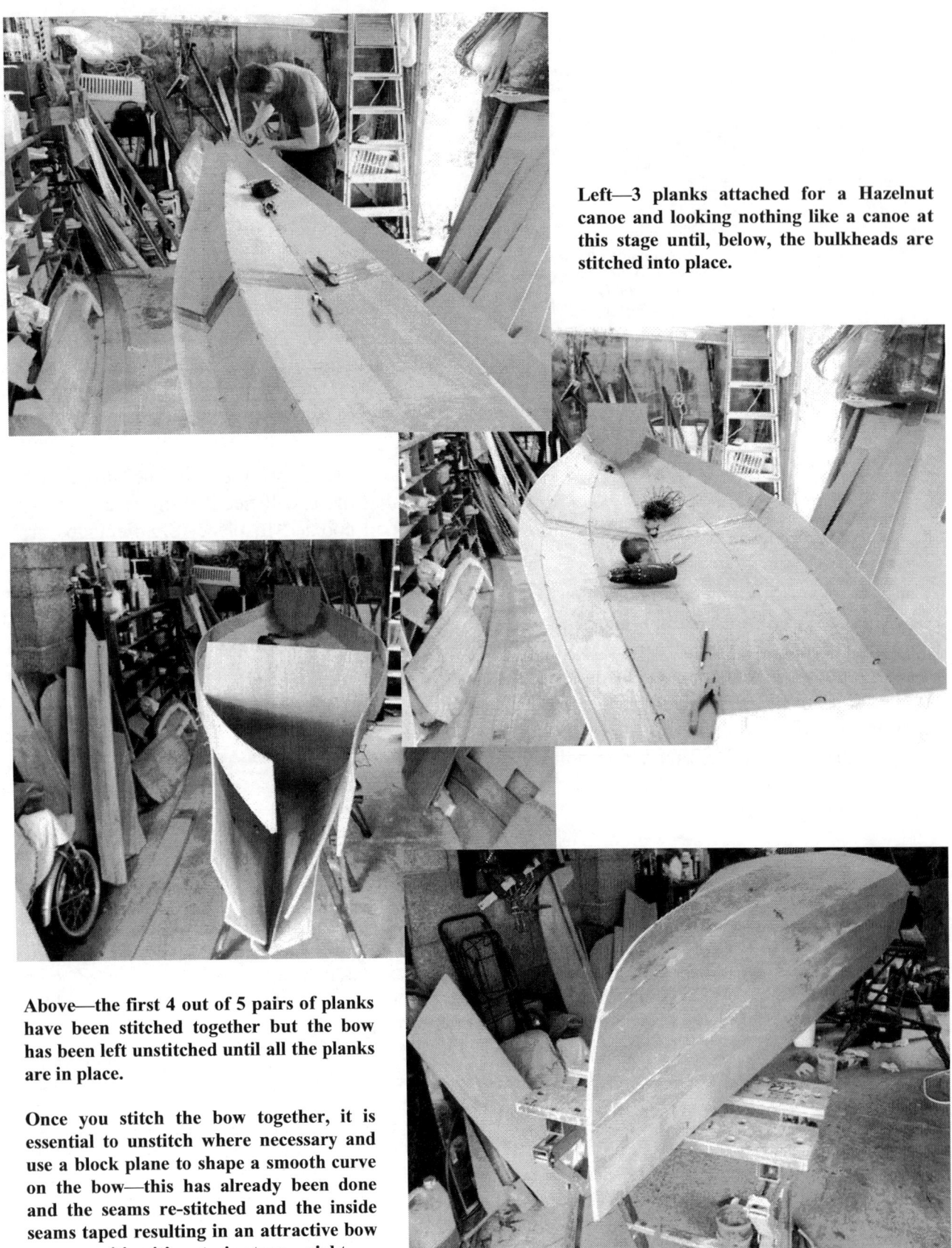

Left—3 planks attached for a Hazelnut canoe and looking nothing like a canoe at this stage until, below, the bulkheads are stitched into place.

Above—the first 4 out of 5 pairs of planks have been stitched together but the bow has been left unstitched until all the planks are in place.

Once you stitch the bow together, it is essential to unstitch where necessary and use a block plane to shape a smooth curve on the bow—this has already been done and the seams re-stitched and the inside seams taped resulting in an attractive bow curve awaiting it's exterior tape—right.

Chapter 7

CHECKING THE SHAPE OF THE BOAT

After you have stitched all the seams together but before the seams have been taped or epoxied, you must check the boat to ensure that it is square and not twisted or out of shape. You must also ensure that bulkheads/frames and seats fit correctly and are not causing any hard spots in the hull skin.

If the hull is twisted, then some bracing will be required to force it into shape whilst the seams are finished. An easy way to check whether there is a twist in the hull, is to sight along the tops of frames/bulkheads and transom to see whether all the top lines of these components are parallel to each other (Figure 28) - or use 'winding' sticks' - photograph on page 36.

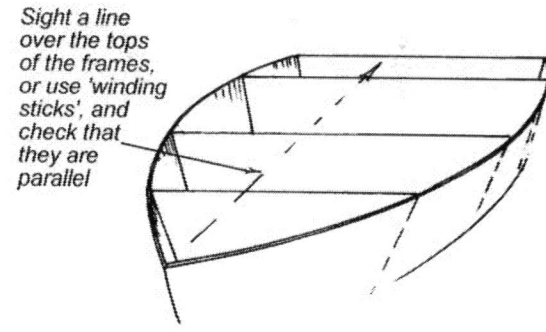

Sight a line over the tops of the frames, or use 'winding sticks', and check that they are parallel

Fig 28. Checking over the tops of the frames to make sure the hull is untwisted.

Measurements can be taken from the stem to the ends of each frame/bulkhead where they meet the hull sides to see whether they are the same both sides and a plumb line can be used to see whether the frames etc., are vertical (Figure 29). Because you have no definite building jig, there is no accurate reference to

Above—2 or 3 lengths of wood batten are used as 'winding sticks' by laying them across the gunwales to check for twist in the hull—if the sticks appear parallel there is no twist.

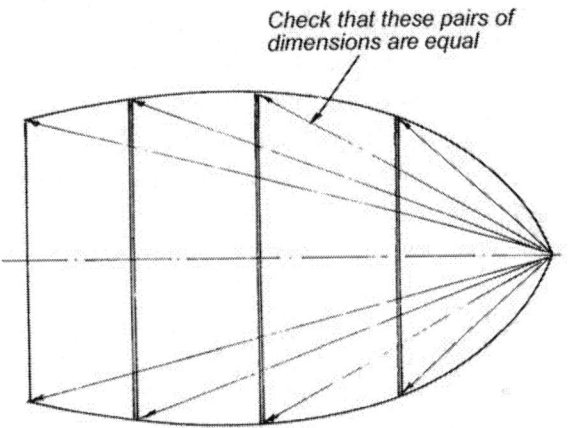

Check that these pairs of dimensions are equal

Fig 29. Using pairs of dimensions to check the shape.

work to, but you can get most components sitting in a level or vertical position by eye and the judicious use of a hammer. You can finally tighten up the wire ties as you do this.

Use scrap timber to brace out gunwales or to force a panel up or down, or in or out by jamming one end against a wall, ceiling or floor with the other end on a hull panel (Figure 30). This latter end should have a ply pad under it to prevent bruising the wood. Heavy weights can also be used to good effect.

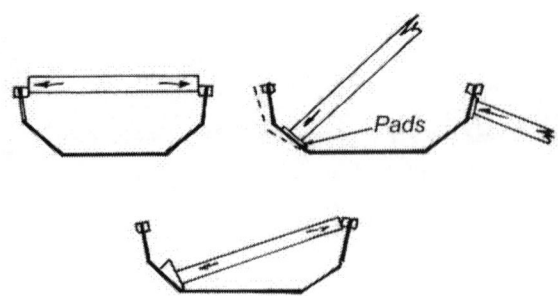

Pads

Fig 30. Pushing the boat into shape.

Remember that towels spread over a stiff area and soaked in boiling water from a kettle will also help, but do not soak the wood too much as it will raise the wood fibres and could weaken the area in the stressed area, especially if you are using low grade baulk cored plywood.

You must also let the wood dry thoroughly whilst it is being held in shape by struts, cramps etc., before using wood glue or resin in the area.

Above—a Gdansk 17' dayboat based on a Polish Fishing Boat—the planks are all stitched together, the frames inserted and the hull checked for twist—she is now ready to have her inside chine seams taped.

Chapter 8

STITCH AND TAPE SEAMS
& EPOXY FILLETING FRAMES ETC IN PLACE

8.1 General

Having stitched all the seams and checked that the hull is untwisted and the correct shape, we can now think about completing the seams to make them structurally sound and waterproof and also, permanently fix the plywood frames, bulkheads and transom into place. Looking at the chine seams first, the process is done, usually both on the inboard and outboard sides of the seams by applying a glass woven roving (WR) tape and soaking it in a resin. The resin 'wets out', that is, soaks through the tape and cures to form a glass/resin matrix which adheres firmly to the plywood and forms a waterproof structural join between the planks.

During the 1960's when stitch and tape boats like the Mirror 11 started to appear on the market, the seams were made up of glass woven roving tape and Polyester type 'A' resin. This resin is still sometimes used due to it's low cost and the ease with which it can often be obtained but, to be honest, I have not used it for many years because although much more expensive, epoxy resins offer many advantages over the Polyester resins.

The advantages of the epoxy resins over the polyester resins are that they adhere much better to the wood, they do not shrink on curing and try and pull away from the wood, they cure harder providing a better surface for higher standards of finish, when soaked into the wood they provide a much better and longer lasting barrier to water etc and are much stronger in tension and compression especially when 'filled' with various modifying powders and will therefore structurally fill gaps and form a very strong glue. They may suffer if subject to ultra-violet light and therefore need protection from direct sunlight and they are a good deal more expensive than Polyester resins. But Polyester resins are still available and are often used for canoe and small dinghy building and so we will look at how they are used first.

8.2 Stitch & Tape using Polyester Resin

As we have already said, Polyester resins are not as strong as epoxy resins and so it is usually necessary to retain the stitches in place whilst the inside of the seams, which are tackled first, are glass taped.

Before applying the WR tape to the inside of the chine seam, prepare the seam first by hammering the wire into the seam so that it presents less of a bump (Figure 31) and by scoring the ply lightly where the tape will go to produce a mechanical bond for the tape (Figure 32).

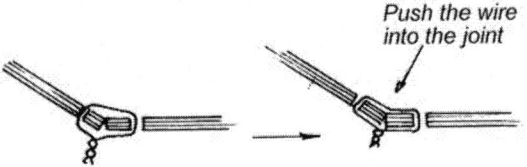

Fig 31. Push the wire into the seam so that it causes a small bump.

Use the edge of a screw driver to do this, a chisel raises the wood fibres too much and prevents the tape from lying down flat. Having done this, prime the surface of the wood with the Polyester (sometimes called fiberglass) resin. Wood soaks up a lot of resin and will drain resin away from the tape

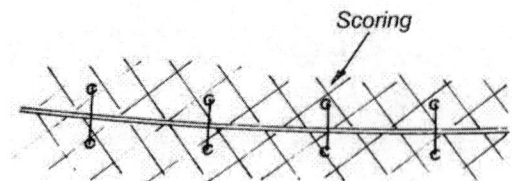

Fig 32. Score the area to increase the mechanical bond between tape and plywood.

causing a weak joint. Allow this priming coat to cure before applying the tape with more resin. The tape should be thoroughly 'wetted' out (soaked) leaving no dry areas. When the tape is good and wet you will note that it changes from it's normally white colour and becomes transparent so that you can see the wood surface through it.

Some builders use rollers for this purpose, but I prefer to use a 1 1/2'' (38mm) brush which allows me to really stipple the resin into the tape. Use brushes which have an unpainted handle as the resin and cleaner will attack the normal paint finish on a brush and the colour will get mixed up with the resin that you apply.

Again, before applying the tape, fill any gaps with a mixture of resin and filler powder (grey talc is the most common) mix in enough to form a thick putty having first put in extra hardener.

When applying the resin primer you may wish to put some masking tape either side of the seam to prevent the resin spreading too far. Take the tape off (by pealing it back on it's self) before the resin has cured (Figure 33).

The resin you should use for the taping is General Purpose Type 'A' resin which usually requires 5cc of catalyst per lb. to harden it (but check the suppliers literature).

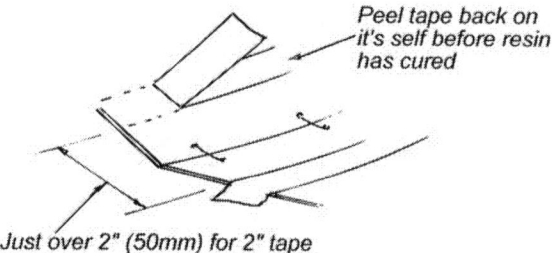

Peel tape back on it's self before resin has cured

Just over 2" (50mm) for 2" tape

Fig 33. Taping each side of the join to prevent resin from spreading too far.

You can use slightly more catalyst, say 8 cc in cold conditions or when you are mixing fillers with the resin and the catalyst should be thoroughly mixed with the resin first before you add the fillers.

I usually make up resin and catalyst in large yogurt cartons. If you fill these to about 3/4 of their volume this is about 3/4 lb of resin, but check this for yourself. Make a large black mark with a crayon on the outside of the carton and you can refill accurately to the same level each time.

When using the resin, keep it on the move in the carton all the time by stirring it with the brush each time you reload the brush. You will find that the heat from your hand will cause the resin in the carton to cure very quickly and stirring it slows this process down. It is sometimes a good idea to pour part of the catalysed resin into a wider container so that you spread it's volume and this will slow it's cure. If you mix up too much resin and catalyst in one go it will cure fast in the container because of the bulk heat reaction.

Make sure that the catalyst is thoroughly mixed through the resin (you usually see the resin change from pink to a darker colour when it is mixed) but do not be tempted to use too much catalyst as I have found that it tends to make the resin too brittle. Use a

special measuring bottle to measure out the catalyst, or a syringe.

Do make sure that you are properly set up before you start with:
- Acetone for cleaning the brushes and yourself.
- Plenty of large yogurt/pot noodle (I am not asking you to eat the stuff!) type containers.
- Mixing sticks.
- Cheap 1'' (25mm) and 1 1/2'' (38mm) brushes.
- Large syringes for measuring out the catalyst.
- Barrier cream and disposable surgical type gloves.

2'' (50mm) 8 oz. tape is sufficient for the seams of boats up to 12' (3.6m) in length made of 1/4'' (6mm) ply. Use 3'' (75mm) tape or 2 layers of slightly overlapping 2'' (50mm) tape for highly stressed areas or 1/4'' (6mm) ply boats over 12' in length (Figure 34).

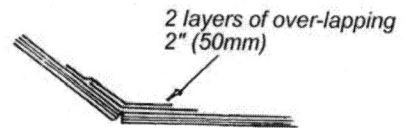

2 layers of over-lapping 2" (50mm)

Fig 34. Using 2 layers of W.R. glass tape on highly stressed areas.

For boats made out of 3/8'' (9mm) ply it is best to use a combination of epoxy resin fillet and several layers of tape (see Figures 44 and 45). I do not use Polyester resin when using plywood over 1/4'' (6mm) thickness.

Once the inside of the seam has cured, turn the boat over and cut the wires off flush with the ply (use snips and a file or a hacksaw blade) (Figure 35). Plane and fill the seam and prepare as for the inside of the seam before applying the tape.

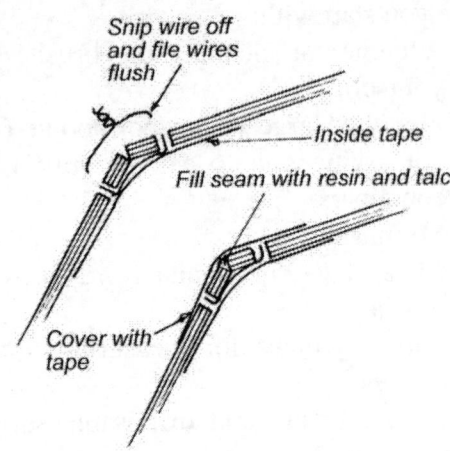

Fig 35. Finishing the outside of the stitch and tape seam.

8.3 Stitch & Tape using Epoxy Resin

8.3.1 For Small Boats & Canoes

Because of the gap filling and glue strength of epoxy resins when they are modified by mixing them with various filler powders, we can often use them to bond the hull planks together so that most of the stitches can be removed before taping begins. This leaves a much neater chine seam but I would not do this with boats that use Polyester resins in their construction. The stitches at the bow which are often under a fair amount of stress are left in place and simply covered when thickened epoxy is applied.

The idea is to 'spot-weld' the panel seams with small amounts of thickened resin in between the stitches. The thickened resin can be applied to both the inside of the seam and to the 'V gap on the outside of the seam—Figure 36. Once this has cured, the stitches can be entirely removed leaving a surface on

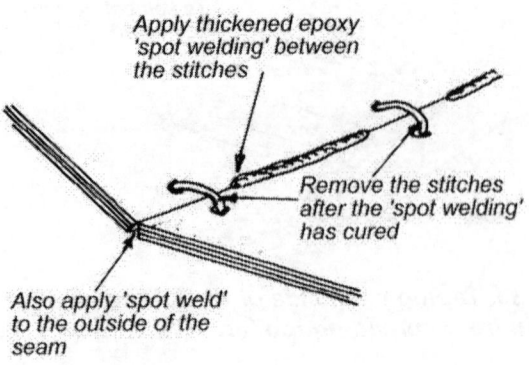

Fig 36. Applying thickened epoxy 'spot welds' to the seam so that the stitches can be removed.

the inside of the seam free of all the stitches which would cause bumps in the glass tape. This process of course, takes more time, but is well worth doing if you want to produce a clean interior.

The equipment required is similar to that used for Polyester resins except that I always use the 'mini pumps' supplied by the resin manufacturer to accurately measure out the resin and hardener which is often in a 5:1 mix of resin to hardener.

Having allowed the epoxy fillets to cure and removed all the stitches, you can, lightly sand down the seams and carefully clean all saw dust and debris out from the interior of the hull. Now, starting with the centerline seam and working your way up, lay out and cut the lengths of glass tape. In most canoes you can remove bulkheads and replace them with braces across the beam to keep the hull in it's correct shape. This allows you to run your chine tapes right through from bow to stern. In dinghies, you may not be able to do this although I have braced the gunwales apart on a dinghy, removed the ply frames, taped the seams and then, before the epoxy has cured, quickly refitted the frames over the tape. But this is not always possible in which case you will need to run your tape in between the frames etc.

Having cut the tape lengths carefully remove and stack the tapes in order leaving you with the centreline tape to hand—*Note, cutting and laying out your tapes this way applies to hulls using Polyester resin too.*

Above—laying out and cutting the W.R. tapes for a Hazelnut canoe.

I find that with most single taped chine seams, there is no need to 'prime' the seam first—so, apply the resin/hardener mix using a brush to the seam and then apply the tape from one end, gently pulling and stretching it into a straight line over the seam. The epoxy resin will start to wet it out and as it does so I quickly go over it with the brush, to help. Do not apply more resin yet but go to the next seam which is the first chine seam and repeat the process there. Having applied the first of the chine seam tapes, go back to the centerline seam tape and apply more resin to it if required to wet it out.

Continue this process until all the chine seams have been taped. Do not apply too much resin or you will end up with resin drips and runs.

Once cured, turn the hull over and fill the outside seams with thickened epoxy, clean up and apply the outside tapes.

Above—the W.R. tape on the centreline seam starting to 'wet out'.

Below—the outside chine seams have been taped and now the tape is being applied to the bow—it has to have cuts each side so that it will go round the curve—the tape is allowed to overlap—these are ground flat later.

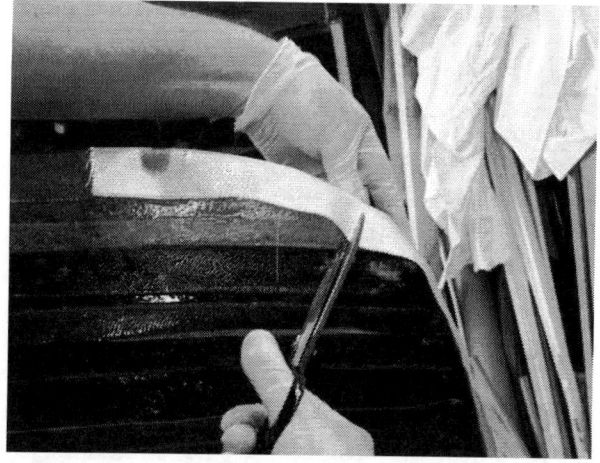

41

8.3.1.1 Omitting the Tapes on the Outside of the Chine Seams

When using epoxies (as opposed to polyester resins) for stitch and tape construction, I have started to omit the glass tape on the outside of chine seams. I have done this on canoes and small dinghies which have more than two chines per side (Figure 37). On small craft which have less than two chines per side, the stress on each chine may be too great not to apply tape on both sides of the chine seams.

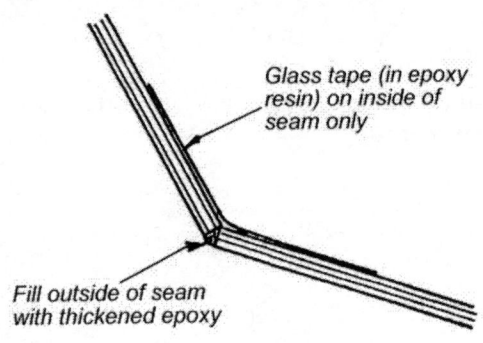

Fig 37. Taping the inside of the chine seam only and simply filling the outside of the seam with thickened epoxy.

Our family canoe for many years was one of my Christine designs which has four planks per side. This craft has given sterling service without any sign of movement in the chine seams despite being dropped and generally mishandled. She has tape on the inside seams and on the outside of the centreline seam only, with the remaining seams on the outside simply filled with thickened epoxy.

Where the hull panels meet each other with no angle, or little angle between them (for instance on the topsides, towards the bow), there is no where to put any thickened epoxy. In this case, a 'groove' of some sort needs to

be created to accommodate the epoxy filleting.

I have done this in one of two ways, either by using a router to create a rebate in the edges of the panels (Figure 38), or by planing a bevel on the edges (Figure 39).

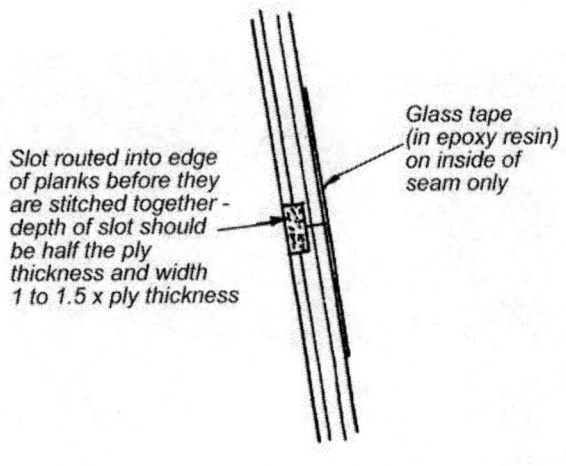

Fig 38. Routed slot used to accommodate the epoxy fillet when the planks are in-line with each other.

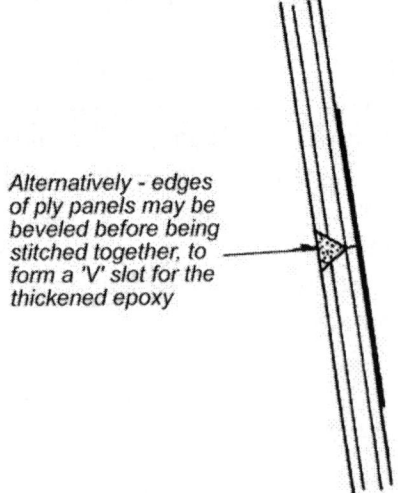

Fig 39. A 'V' gap used for the same purpose.

You can sometimes gauge whether the planking will need a slot, from the shape of the forward frame or bulkhead given on the plans. However, the only true way to see where this maybe necessary, is to stitch the panels together first. This will mean unstitching in order to route or plane the groove up. Do not try routing 'on the job' with the planks stitched up! I have tried this and the router insists on taking any route but the one you want it to take. So take the time to unstitch before attempting to router or plane.

8.3.1.2 Eliminating Tape Bumps on the Outside of the Chine Seam

Where, due to it's size or type, a boat definitely needs tapes on the outside of the chines, I often get asked whether it is possible to construct a stitch and tape craft without having the 'bump' created by the glass tape on the chine seams.

On boats which are built from 9mm (3/8") or thicker plywood, the outside veneer of the ply panel can be removed over an area which will accommodate the glass tape (Figure 40). This is best done using a router set to a depth which will remove the outside veneer and over a width slightly more than half the width of the tape being used. If more than one layer of tape is to be used, then the amount of plywood to be removed might be a little more but do not over do this or you will loose much of the strength in the plywood.

The bump created by a glass tape which has not been set into a routed area to accept the tape and sits on top of the plywood can be more or less eliminated by the careful use of fillers—see Chapter 11.

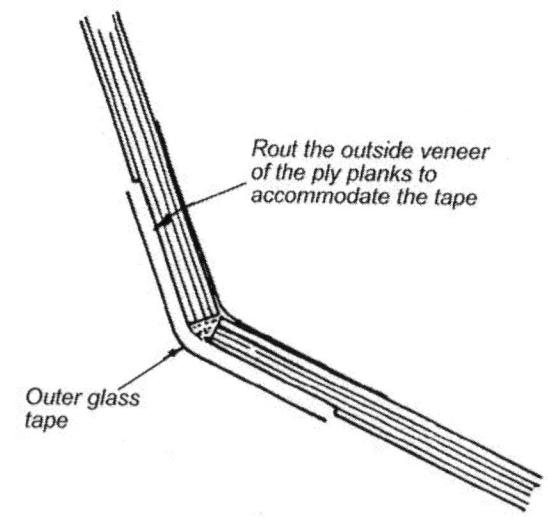

Rout the outside veneer of the ply planks to accommodate the tape

Outer glass tape

Fig 40. Routing away the outside veneer so that the tape can sit flush with the plywood.

Above—the chine seams of a Highlander 18 routed out ready to receive the chine tape.

8.3.2 For Larger Boats

Above 18' (5.5m) and for boats below this length which are going to be used in tough conditions then you cannot avoid using 3/8'' (9mm) ply for the hull skin and this requires a more complex form of stitch and tape joint to that used on 1/4'' (6mm) ply boats. Basically, the inside of the seam is reinforced with an epoxy fillet and the seam over laid with tape (Figure 41). For boats of around 12' (3.7m) in length and with 3/8'' ply panels the epoxy fillet can be used by itself.

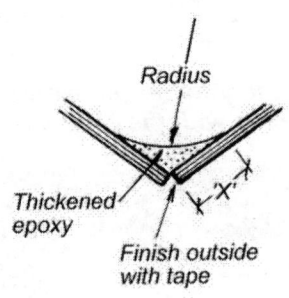

Fig 41. Epoxy fillet sizes—see table below.

Ply Thickness	Radius 'X' for Low Stress	Radius 'X' for High Stress
3mm (1/8")	9mm (3/8")	12mm (1/2")
4mm	12mm (1/2")	15mm (5/8")
6mm (1/4")	18mm (3/4")	25mm (1")
9mm (3/8")	28mm (1 1/8")	36mm (1 1/2")

Epoxy fillets are defined by 2 factors, density and radius. High density fillets are used where strength is required ie. around centerboard cases, bow seams, bulkheads and chine seams and the fillet consists of epoxy resin mixed with various fillers. I tend to use a mixture of Microfibres (WEST 403), Colloidal Silica (WEST 406) to help the fillet flow and Microballoons or High density filler (WEST 404). I use roughly equal amounts of the Microfibres and High density filler with a smaller amount of the Colloidal Silica.

WEST407 which is a lightweight filler works well in most applications as a filler for epoxy glue and for fairing—this is a blend of several different fillers. This is mixed with the resin until you get a fairly thick mixture of ''Mayonnaise'' consistency which will hold it's shape in a lump but where peaks will slowly fall over (Figure 42).

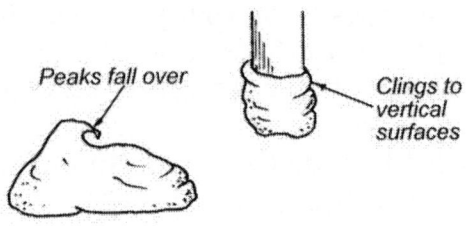

Fig 42. The test of a good filleting mix.

If you do not use WEST407, low density fillets are made to the same consistency or slightly thicker and are made up using Microfibres and Microballoons. This type of fillet material is used for fairing and filling of the seams and is easy to sand.

The radius of the fillet dictates it's size and strength and of course the larger the radius, the greater it's bonding area and therefore the greater it's strength. However, where there is a very obtuse (shallow) angle between the hull panels at a ply seam even a large radius fillet will not give a very strong fillet and therefore it is often better to specify the fillet by it's depth. A figure of at least 1.5 times the thickness of ply being bonded is often used and I have certainly found this to be adequate, so that 3/8'' (9mm) ply would be bonded with a 9/16'' (14mm) deep fillet Figure 43).

For boats of around 15' to 18' this would then be over laid with a layer of 4'' (100mm) wide fibreglass tape which means that the

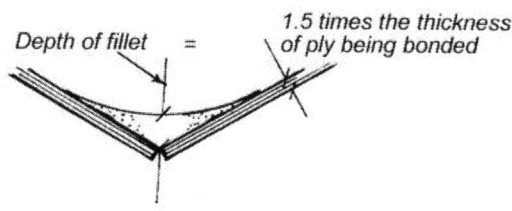

Fig 43. Specifying the size of the epoxy fillet by it's depth.

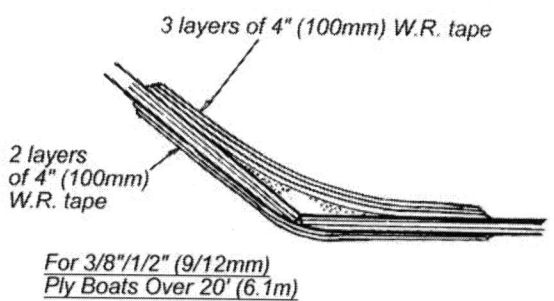

For 3/8"/1/2" (9/12mm)
Ply Boats Over 20' (6.1m)

Fig 45. Epoxy/glass seam construction for boats over 20' using 3/8"/1/2" ply.

fillet needs to be applied with care using perhaps a little more Coloidal Silica in the mix to make it as smooth as possible so that the tape will lie on it without having to bridge humps and hollows (Figure 44). The fillet can be attacked with a grinder to make it smooth but for the sake of your own health, it is a good idea to keep the amount of grinding that you down to a minimum (even with a mask).

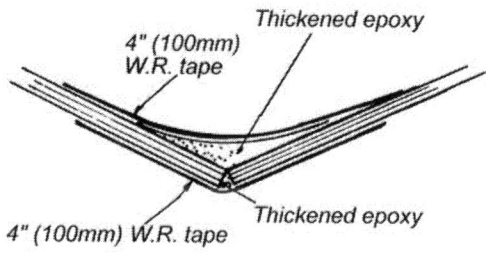

For Dinghies/dayboats 15'-18' (4.6-5.5m)
(For heavy duty boats around 18' (5.5m
use 2 layers of tape inside and out)

Fig 44. Epoxy/glass seam construction for 15'-18' Dinghies and Dayboats.

Boats above 20' (6m) and those carrying a ballast keel should have their epoxy fillets over laid with 3 layers of 4'' (100mm) wide tape with the outside of the chine seam well rounded, filled and covered with 2 layers of 4'' tape (Figure 45). If 4'' tape is unobtainable then it will need to be cut from 8 oz. W.R. cloth. The epoxy fillets for bonding in bulkheads and centreboard cases should have the same size and lay up. The

bailing wire used to stitch the panels together in this size of boat can be removed after the inside fillet has cured by heating the ends of the wire with a small gas torch until the ends are red hot. The heat travels into the seam and melts the resin around the wire allowing it to be withdrawn.

After a little practice, good, smooth, clean fillets can be achieved but there are one or two points which will make this process easier. First, do not try to over thicken the fillet in order to gain more filleting material. This simply starves the joint of resin making it weaker and rougher. Secondly, have a range of different sizes of spatula ready with radiused ends (you can either buy them or make them up from scrap ply/plastic).

Next, apply masking tape to the ply either side of the joint before you apply the epoxy. Although this may sound like extra expense and effort, the result is well worth it and if you have ever looked at professionally built boats and wondered how they achieved such smooth, straight and uniform fillets, taping the seam either side is how they do it. The tape should be removed before the epoxy cures and I do this carefully by pealing it back on itself straight after I have finished applying the epoxy fillet. Put the tape on before you prime the seam (Figure 46).

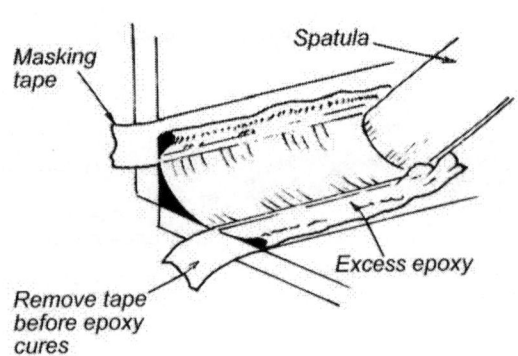

Fig 46. Making a neat epoxy seam.

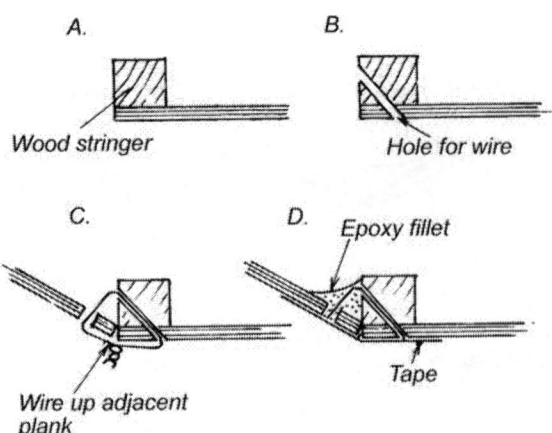

Fig 47. making a 'combi-seam' chine.

Two other things you can do. Use a chisel to carefully scrape off any excess epoxy (especially if you have not used tape) but without digging the chisel into the wood and go over the fillet if it appears rough whilst it cures, with a rounded knife to smooth down bumps.

8.3.3 Combination Seam Joints

Between 12' and 18' (3.8-5.5m) in boat length, rather than increase the thickness of ply used from 1/4'' to 3/8'' which increases the weight and cost by more than 50% when you take into account the structure needed to support it, I often use what I call a combi-seam (Figure 47).

The idea is to increase the stiffness of the ply skin without having to resort to an internal structure that requires time consuming beveling. For 12' to 14' boats glue and nail a 5/8''x5/8'' (15x15mm) Douglas Fir stringer onto the top edge of the lower ply panel and pre-drill as before for the wire ties. Then mate and wire it with the other panel in the usual way. Following this, the 'V' gap is primed with epoxy resin and filled with thickened epoxy (in this case, before the priming resin has cured).

The outside of the seam is finished as before using polyester or epoxy resin for the tape. This creates a very stiff structure within the boat compensating for the thinner ply which can also have intermediate stringers glued and nailed to it between the chines to further stiffen it. For boats of between 15' and 18' use a 3/4''x3/4'' (18x18mm) stringer.

8.3.4 Bonding Plywood Frames to the Hull

Once the chine seams have been taped we can bond the plywood frames/bulkheads into place. Note, that if a ply frame is bisected by a centerboard case, the centerboard and frame is fitted to the boat as one unit—see Chapter 9 for further notes on fitting a centerboard case. I like to fit the ply frames over the taped seams, but if this is not possible, the chine tapes simply need to stop either side of the ply frame. In any case, the epoxy fillets used to bond the frames in place (Figure 48) are applied over the chine seam tape.

See the table on Page 44 for the size of these fillets. More often than not, I leave the stitches holding the frames to the hull, in place as the hull panels often try to pull away from the frame—the epoxy fillet simply hides these stitches.

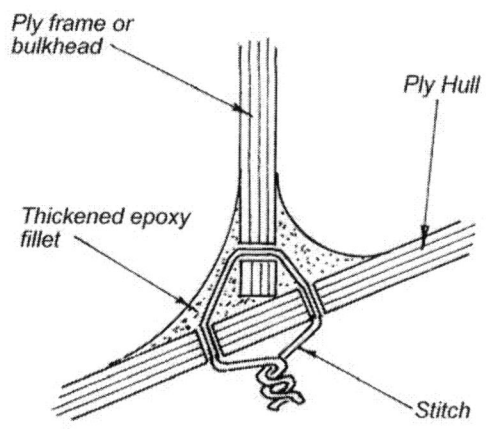

Ply frame or bulkhead

Ply Hull

Thickened epoxy fillet

Stitch

Fig 48. Epoxy filleting frames into the hull.

If the stem and transom are also epoxy filleted in place, this is the time to do this job, again applying the fillets over the ends of the chine seam tapes.

8.3.5 General Notes on Epoxy & Bonding with Epoxy

Firstly one or two general points regarding epoxies. They are fairly high tech' materials and have been designed to be used in more or less ideal conditions. If you are building a boat from scratch with new timber, this should present few problems as the wood that you will be using should have a moisture content of around 12% anyway. Most epoxies are mixed together in a 1:5 ratio of hardener to resin by weight. This mix should not be deviated from and care should be taken in measuring out the quantities. When I am working on dinghies up to around 12' in length, I use 24 ml syringes and use no more than 5 syringe fulls of resin at each mix and sometimes only 3 syringe fulls. For larger quantities, use pumps on the resin containers. To keep the syringes workable, I leave them with the piston drawn half way up the syringe

and with a piece of brass wire in the nozzle.

Epoxies should be used in dry conditions of low humidity (below 65%) where a temperature of around 15 C (60 F) can be maintained. I have worked in conditions with epoxies which have been far from ideal but be careful and if you have any doubt, contact the manufacturer's for advice.

For most applications, I find that using the resin with a fast hardener is fine if the temperature is not too high. The slow hardener allows you more time for adjustment and for rectifying mistakes. The advantage of the fast hardener is that it has a workable cure of around 6 hours.

To keep costs down, I tend to use Marine adhesives (Cascamite, Aerolite 306, Balcotan etc) for most gluing jobs. Using conventional glues for gunwales, thwarts, knees etc is perfectly alright but you may wish to take advantage of the high strength and gap filling properties of epoxies for bonding and gluing items which are subjected to high stress. Mast steps, centreboard/daggerboard cases, engine beds, scarf or butt joints in hull panels and stringers are candidates for this type of treatment.

The process is quite simple. First, dry fit the components together, make sure they fit and devise a way of clamping them whilst the epoxy cures. Next, prime all surfaces with epoxy resin and then apply thickened resin as the glue. The resin is simply thickened with a small amount of Microfibres until a "Ketchup" constancy is achieved which sags and will not hold a shape when it is moved around in the mixing pot.

Bring the components together and clamp lightly until the mixture squeezes out. The epoxy has the advantage over other adhesives in that it will fill gaps in construction and does not need high clamping forces. If you are bonding a very porous wood such as balsa, cedar or spruce, pre-coat the surfaces and let them cure before applying the priming coat and thickened resin. Likewise, if you are bonding the end grain of wood and the surface appears dry and flat, then this will need pre coating.

If you have large gaps in the joint, then the resin should be thicker. Any clamping system can be employed which produces even pressure over the whole surface and I often use rope, string and rubber cut from old inner tubes. The components tend to slip over each other more easily with the epoxy than they may do with ordinary adhesives and I therefore find on thin ply, that it is a good idea to use 1 or 2 staples to prevent this. On larger components, even though they are not needed for strength, screws which have been tried at the dry fit stage are also very helpful to keep the components in their correct position.

For components like centreboard case logs, it is a good idea to make a gap for the epoxy to sit in (Figure 49). This ensures a strong joint through and through with no possibility of epoxy starvation. Therefore the faces of the logs should be slightly bevelled and the subsequent gap produced against the case side primed and filled with thickened epoxy.

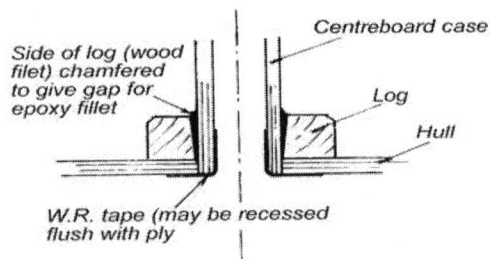

Fig 49. Epoxy filleting centerboard case logs in place.

Such items also benefit from an epoxy fillet applied in the same way as the fillets in chine seams because this makes the bonding area larger and spreads the loads (Figure 50).

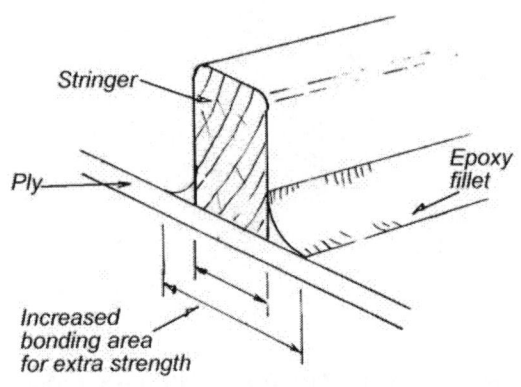

Fig 50. Increasing bonding area for additional strength.

Above—Chris Bennett's neatly taped example of a Highlander 7'6" dinghy ready for finishing.

Chapter 9

FITTING OUT THE HULL
WITH THWARTS, CENTREBOARD, DECKING ETC

9.1 General

Having completed at least the inside of the chine (plank) seams and bonded in the plywood frames, we can start to look fitting the hull out with thwarts (seats), decking etc. All of these components will, in a modern stitch and tape design, have the secondary function of adding strength and stiffness to the hull and I usually start with the component which adds most to the stiffness of the hull and that is the gunwales.

9.2 The Gunwales

The gunwales are the longitudinal pieces of wood attached to the top edge of the plywood planking. They often consist of two pieces, the 'inwales' on the inboard side of the planking and the 'outwale' on the outboard side of the planking and together, they sandwich the top edge of the uppermost plank. On simple boats, this edge is sanded and varnished or painted but, in some boats, the gunwale may have a wood cap covering the gunwale as well.

9.2.1 The Inwales

9.2.1.1 Simple Solid Inwales

The simplest inwale is a strip of wood attached directly to the inboard side of the top plank. The wood strip needs to be long enough to stretch from the bow to the transom (or stern post in a double ended boat) - if you cannot get wood this length then you must scarf two pieces together (see the

Appendices) - do not try to join two pieces of wood on the boat as you fit the inwale—always make the join before trying to fit the inwale.

Most often, the bow end of the inwale is covered by decking or a breasthook (triangular knee at the bow) and so getting a close and neat join between the port and starboard inwales is not necessary. I lay the end of one inwale on the edge of the boat and mark what I estimate to be the required shape of the front end cut this and offer it up to the boat. Holding it in place is difficult but clamp it in place as best you can.

Having got the correct shape at the bow end, I then spring the inwale into place until it overhangs the transom and mark this end. Getting the aft end correct is more important because it is often left exposed (Figure 51).

At the transom, the plans will often call for quarter knees to be fitted—either from solid wood on the face of the inwale or from plywood triangles fastened to the under side or topside of the inwale—Figure 52.

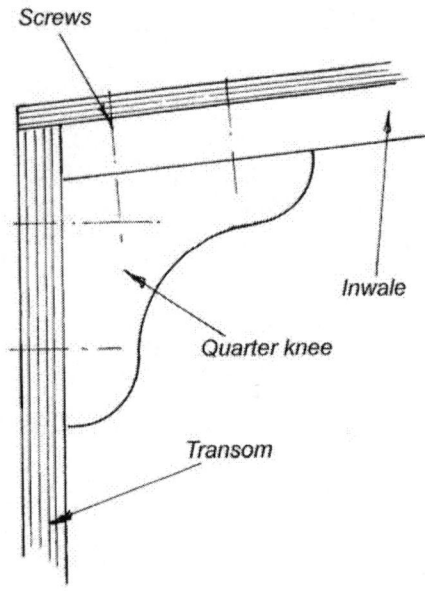

Fig 52. A 'solid' wood quarter knee—make up a hardboard template to get the correct shape.

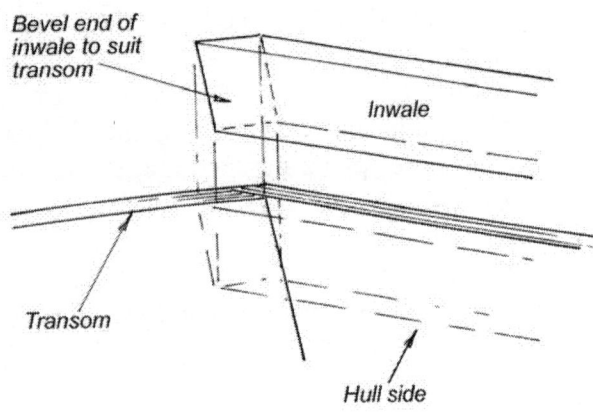

Fig 51. Shaping the aft end of the inwale.

Having fitted one inwale, I screw this in place (from the outside of the ply plank) and cut and fit the inwale on the opposite side again screwing it into place. Mark across the top edge of the plank and inwales at various different places so that when you remove and apply glue, you can get the inwales back into their correct positions.

Above—the inwales and upper plank have been cut down to accept a plywood breasthook which will cover the ends of the inwale—this could be taken further back to form a proper foredeck—cutting the inwale and plank down allow the breasthook to lie flush with the top of the gunwale—Figure 53.

As already mentioned, the front end of the inwales may be covered with a plywood deck or breasthook which may simply be 'planted' directly on top of the gunwales but, to cover the exposed edge of the plywood, it may also be set down 'flush' with the top of the gunwale. This makes a much neater job (Figure 53).

The pictures below show the stages of fitting a 'flush' deck or breasthook—first the inwale and plank edge are cut down by the thickness of the ply used for the deck/breasthook, in this case using a jig-saw—the ply deck/breasthook is then fitted oversize and planed back flush with the hull side and finally, the outwale is fitted to cover the exposed edge of the plywood.

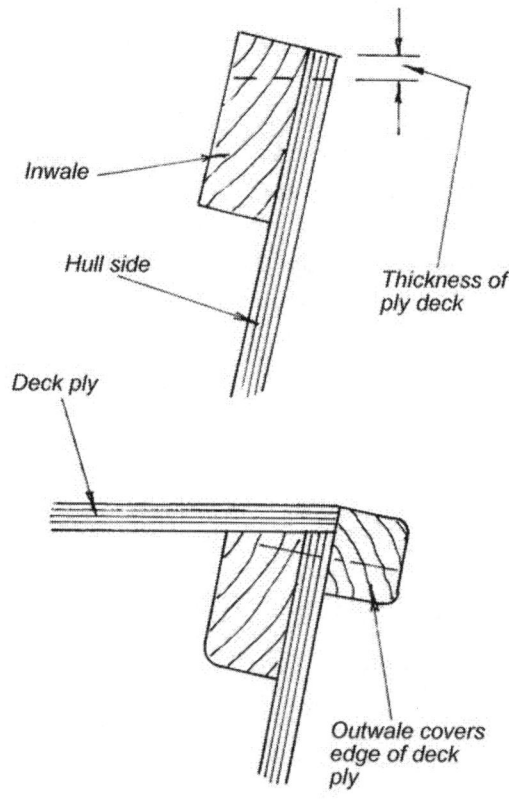

Fig 53. Setting a plywood deck or breasthook down flush with the top of the gunwale to cover the exposed edge of the plywood.

9.2.1.2 Open Pattern Inwales

Open pattern inwales have the inwale stringer itself spaced away from the top edge of the plank by spacer blocks (Figure 54). Why do this? Well, it will stiffen the gunwale further and it also allows all the water to be drained from a boat when tipping it on it's side as there is space between the inwale and the hull side. It is also part of a method of building where the inwale was often fitted to the inboard faces of the small steamed timbers used in some traditionally built boats. Some builders stop the open gunwale at the quarter knees and breast hook and just 'let' it into them by cutting a slot for it, but I prefer the method shown in Figure 54 where it is allowed to butt against the transom and inner stem. At these points the spacer blocks are long enough to match the lengths of the quarter knees and breast hook.

The first task is to cut all the spacer blocks and to hold them to the planking using strong tape. The inwale can now be carefully cut to length – use bevel gauges and careful measuring to get the angles of the ends correct. You may want to shape one end first and screw it in place at that end and through 2 or 3 further spacer blocks so that it is positioned correctly. Screw through from the outside of the plywood plank (Figure 55). Whilst this one end is secure, you can bend the inwale round and cut the other end to suit. Finally, you can secure it along it's length by screwing through each spacer block. I prefer to do both sides together to lessen the risk of distorting the overall gunwale shape of the boat.

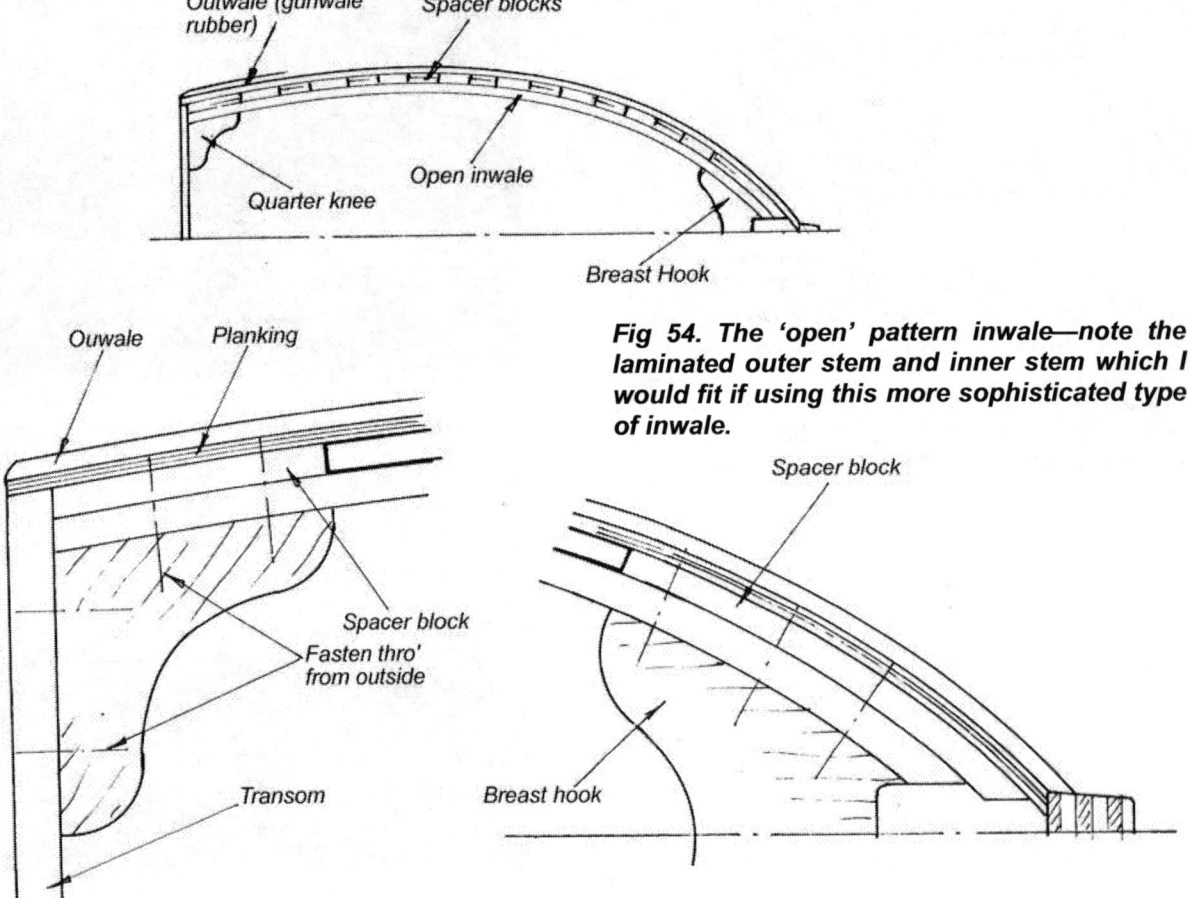

Fig 54. The 'open' pattern inwale—note the laminated outer stem and inner stem which I would fit if using this more sophisticated type of inwale.

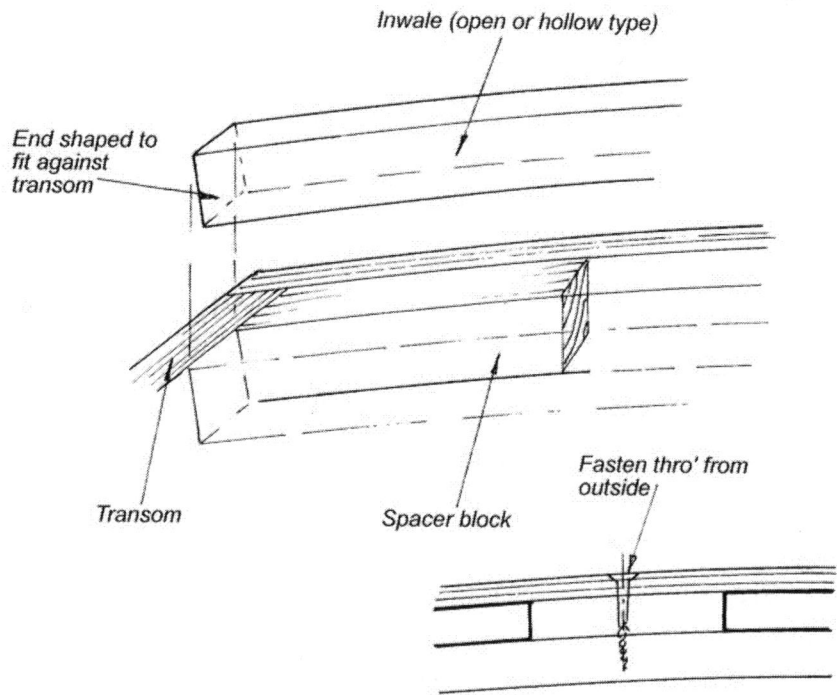

Inwale (open or hollow type)

End shaped to
fit against
transom

Transom

Spacer block

Fasten thro' from
outside

**Fig 55. Fixing the open type
inwale to the aft end.**

Now remove the inwales with their spacer blocks and sand each block, putting a round onto the corners at each end. The inwale and spacers can now be glued and screwed back in place.

9.2.2 The Outwales

These are simply glued and screwed to the outside of the top edge of the uppermost plank sandwiching the plank with the inwale (Figure 53). I screw right through to the inwale at approximately 10" (250mm) centres and fill over the screw heads with thickened epoxy. Make sure that the ends of the outwales are well bevelled.

9.3 Solid Quarter Knees and Breast Hook

We mentioned quarter knees on Page 50—these may be simple triangular pieces of plywood of the same thickness as the hull planking epoxied to the inwale and transom but we may want something more sophisticated than that and use thicker solid wood.

With the inwales in place we can take hardboard patterns off the boat for the quarter knees and breast hook. Use hardboard for the patterns – offer a piece up, mark it out roughly for the lines between the inwale and transom for the quarter knees and the lines between port and starboard inwales and the inner stem, for the breast hook. It is important to orientate the grain on solid wood knees correctly (Figure 56).

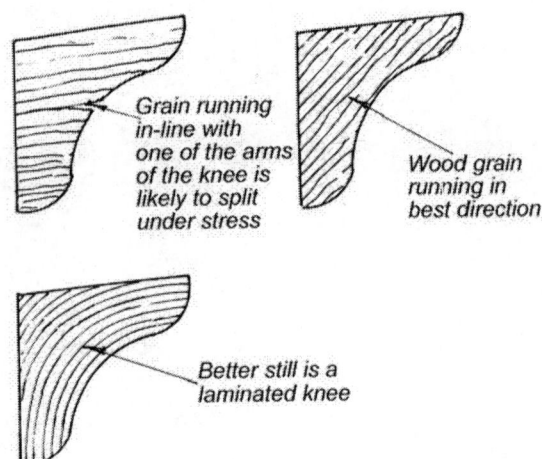

Fig 56. The Solid Wood Quarter Knee.

The edges of both the quarter knees and breast hook will have to be slightly bevelled to suit the vertical angle of the inwale so, once they have been cut out, carefully plane the edges to suit using a bevel gauge to help (Figure 57).

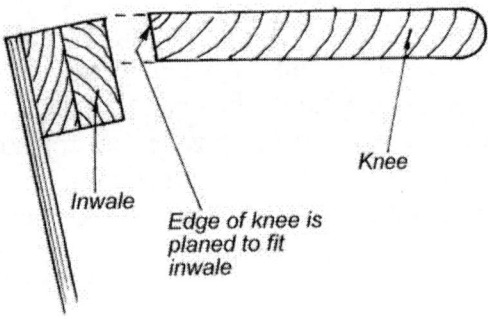

Fig 57. Fitting the quarter knee to the inwale.

The quarter knees and breast hook can now be glued in place and screwed through from the outside.

9.4 Taking Shapes off the Boat & Fitting Thwarts (Seats)

Having stiffened the hull with the gunwales, we are at a stage where we may need to take

shapes from the boat for intermediate bulkheads and horizontal surfaces like thwarts (seats) and buoyancy chambers etc.

You may also need to check the dimensions given to you on the plans for frames etc because different makes of plywood bend in different ways, and therefore it is impossible to give accurate measurements for some components on the drawings. Taking these measurements is quite easy and if epoxy fillet or taped seams are being used, gaps that may occur can be filled and will not matter.

Always measure to reference lines and points ie., the centreline of the boat, or a gunwale or frame line. Locate the position of the item you are working on in the boat from dimensions given on the drawings. These dimensions usually give the position of a frame at the gunwale level, therefore put a batten across the boat at this point and check that it is square to the centreline by taking measurements both sides to the stem and altering the way that the batten lies until they are equal (see Figure 29).

Fix the batten temporarily in place with tape and then use a plumb line (a piece of light string with a weight tied to it's lower end so that when it is suspended, the line will be vertical) to spot this position around the inside of the hull (Figure 58).

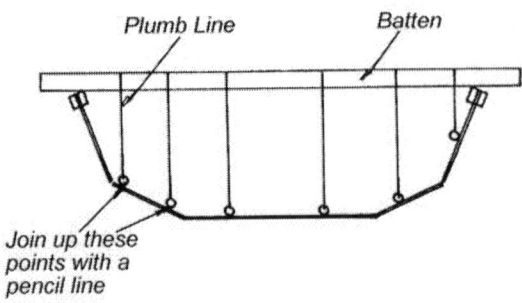

Fig 58. Marking the position of a frame on the inside of the hull.

You must of course ensure that the hull is level both fore and aft and athwartships (across the boat) before you start. Use a large carpenter's level to do this, or a long thin transparent tube filled with water (Figure 59).

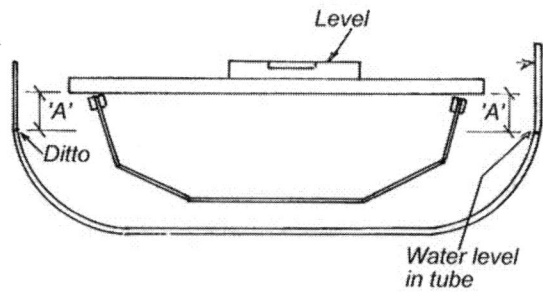

Fig 59. Leveling the hull.

Measurements using a tape, plumb line and level can then be taken (Figure 60).

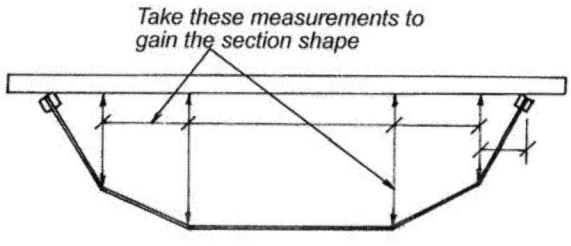

Fig 60. Taking vertical and horizontal measurements to define a frame shape.

For side seats or items which are horizontal, use the edge of the seat as a reference line. Using a square and level, take the measurements which can then be plotted onto the ply (Figure 61).

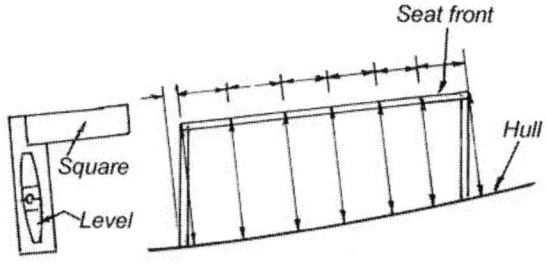

Fig 61. Taking measurements for a side bench top.

For safety, I still prefer to cut the ply slightly oversize and to finally trim it to shape on the boat. For awkward and tricky shapes, a stiff card or hardboard template can be made up.

Take the width measurements for the forward and aft edge of the thwarts from the hull (pinch rods are good for this—Fig 62) and transfer these to the plank stock you are using for the thwarts. When cutting the shape allow for any curve that there might be in the hull side (Figure 62).

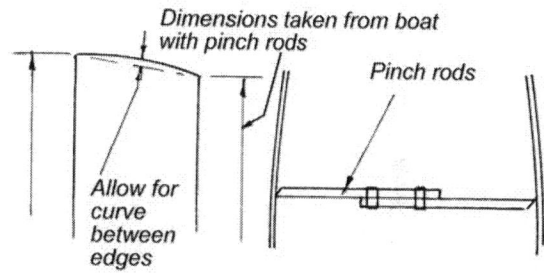

Fig 62. taking the width of the thwarts/seats from the boat.

Side benches can be tackled in 2 or 3 ways – the most common are plank and open (battened) benches (Figure 63). The latter are easily fitted and usually the ends of the battens simply rest on top of the thwarts and are screwed to them. The plank type of side bench is shaped to the side of the hull and it is let into the thwarts rather than just being butted to them (Figure 64). Take the shape from the boat using the method shown in Figure 61.

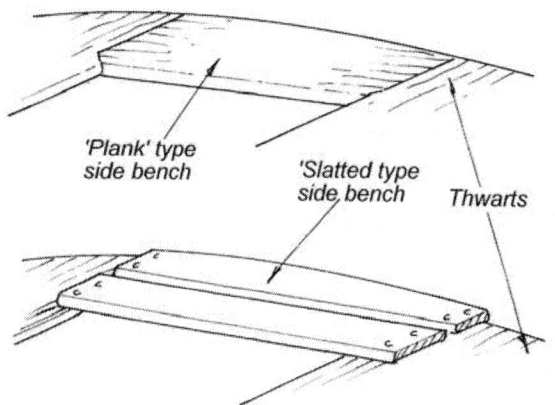

Fig 63. Side benches.

55

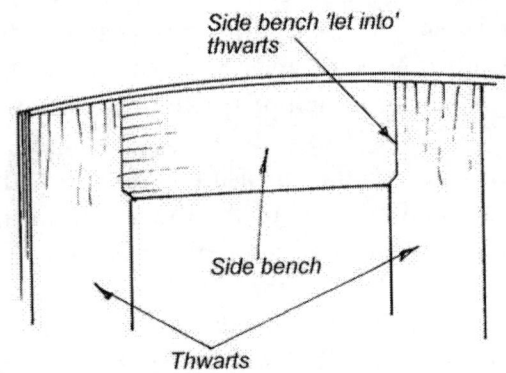

Fig 64. Ply or solid wood side bench tops 'let' into athwartship seats.

Side bench seats often need a supporting hanging knee underneath, of either plywood or solid wood – (Figure 65). Simple plywood seats and thwarts will require supporting wood fillets under their edges to make them stiff—having shaped the plywood seat top I then fit the supporting fillets off the boat to the seat before fitting the whole assembly to the hull.

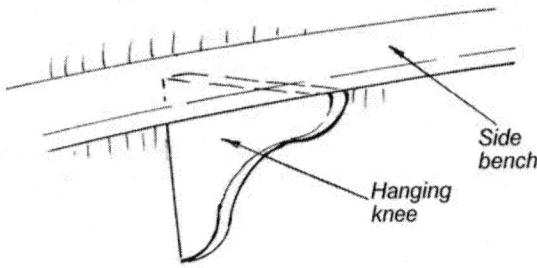

Fig 65. Side bench supporting hanging knee.

9.5 Centreboards & Daggerboards

9.5.1 The Case

There are various ways in which cases are made up and fitted to the hull – Figure 66 gives some typical examples of the join

between hull and case. There are a couple of important points to consider including the strength of the join, the leak-proofness of the join and the accuracy with which the case is aligned with the hull.

The case needs to be fitted to the hull accurately so that the case is vertical and on the centreline. Make sure that the hull is set up level before you fit the case. Dry fit the case to the hull, mark around it onto the hull, remove the case and drill holes where the ends of the slot through the hull will occur. Cut the slot with a jig-saw or hole saw and clean up the edges carefully. Any exposed edges of ply will need to be carefully filled with epoxy so that water cannot soak onto the plywood.

There are one or two points to take into consideration in it's construction. First, the interior surfaces will be hidden and therefore must be 'finished' with whatever epoxy coating/sheathing etc they are to receive before final assembly and secondly, the plywood used for the sides tends to warp during construction and fitting and so the

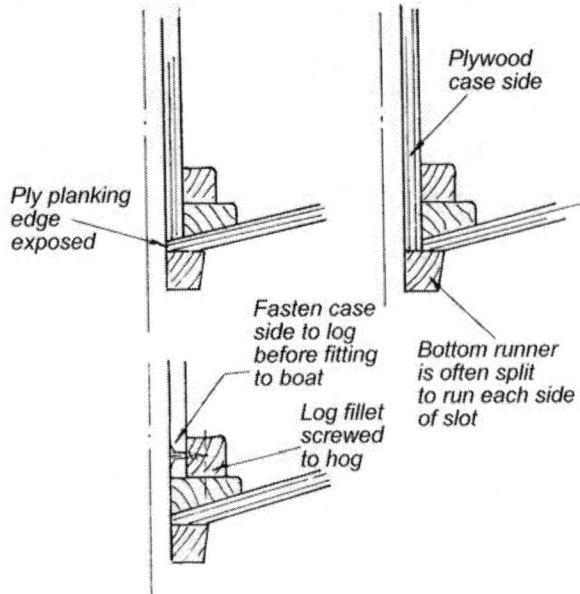

Fig 66. Different ways of fitting centerboard/ daggerboard cases.

case ends up with the gap between the sides narrower in the centre than it is at the ends – temporary battens fitted during the installation stage help prevent this (Figure 67).

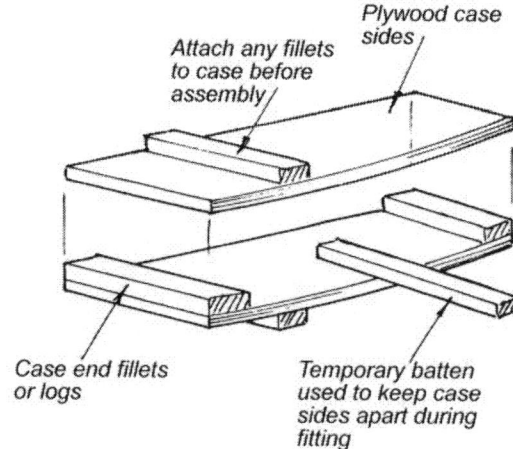

Fig 67. Preparing centreboard case sides.

A centreboard case will often have a cap – make sure that this is dry screwed in place and not glued so that it can be removed later if required to get at the centreboard (Figure 68).

Above—the daggerboard case with it's knees, made as a separate unit and ready to fit into a Highlander 7'6" by Chris Bennett.

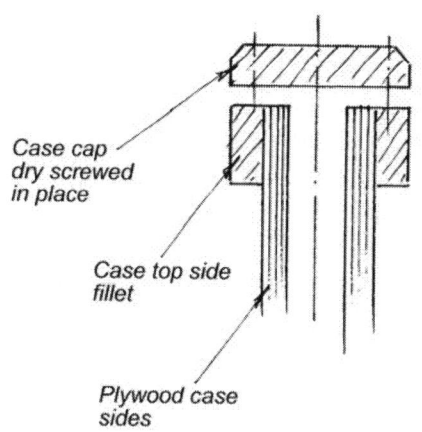

Fig 68. The centerboard case cap.

9.5.2 The Centre/Daggerboard

The board should be detailed on the drawings – do remember that it's job is to produce a force which counteracts the force component produced by the sails, that pushes the boat sideways – to do this with maximum efficiency it needs to be carefully shaped. Boards on simple knock about boats often have all their edges rounded, but for more sophisticated boats the board in it's section, should get as close to a proper hydrofoil type shape as possible with a rounded and slightly tapered leading edge and a tapered trailing edge (Figure 69). Assuming that the board is made of plywood, make sure that it is well coated with epoxy – it may also be sheathed with woven roving too and the thickness of this should be taken account of, so that the completed board does not jam in the case.

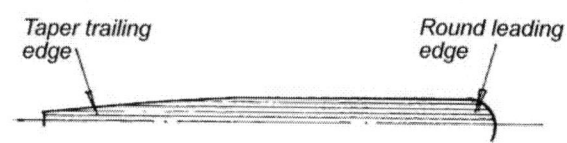

Fig 69. Shaping a simple plywood board.

9.5.3 Fitting Pivots

Figure 70 shows a section through a typical centreboard pivot. Note that the case sides are reinforced with a second thickness of plywood or hardwood and that the pivot has large 'penny' washers each side. Use a 'Nyloc' nut or two locking nuts so that the pivot bolt cannot unscrew itself and use a Marine Sealant when fitting to cut down leaks. Make sure that the holes drilled through the case sides for the pivot are well sealed with epoxy.

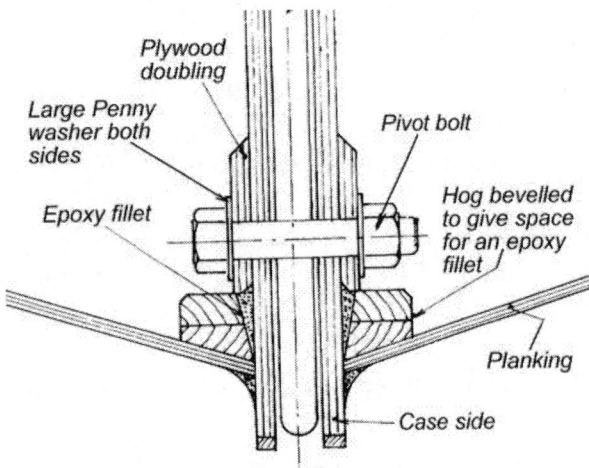

Fig 70. The centerboard pivot—this example also shows another way of fitting the case.

9.5.4 Combined Case & Frame

If the centreboard/daggerboard case bisects a frame it will need to be fitted with the frame as a combined unit. The easiest way to do this is to make up the frame by itself first as a complete unit (un-cut for the case) and fit this dry in the hull whilst you complete the hull shell, and then remove it and cut it to fit with the case before refitting the combined unit, into the hull.

Figure 67 shows a typical case with fillets on it's side to which the frame would be attached—make sure that the fillets are attached to the case sides and screwed through from the inboard faces of the case before the case is assembled.

Above—the centreboard case of a Stornoway 14 by Ian Parsons made up as a unit and ready to be fitted together with other pieces of the fore and aft girder and frames before having planks fitted.

Some stitch and tape designs like the Selway Fisher Stornoway 14 and 16 have a fore and aft central girder which includes the centreboard case and which is assembled with the transom and frames before the planks are attached—care needs to be taken using the Centreline and Datum Line to assemble all these components accurately.

Above—the centreboard case attached to the mid frame of a Stornoway 12 and fitted to the hull.

9.6 The Decking

9.6.1 The Deck Structure

Very often any decking on a simple stitch and tape boat is flat without a camber (The curvature seen on the decking of many boats that produces a 'peak' in the centre of the deck.

However, a cambered deck is very attractive and helps stiffen the boat and allows water to run off the deck easier. The following notes on building a cambered deck also apply to a flat deck. We will assume that the tops of any athwartship (side to side) plywood frames/bulkheads have been cut over height leaving material to be trimmed. For the main deck there are 2 important items to consider – the position of the carlin which defines the plan shape of the cockpit coaming and the shape of the beams (Figure 71).

I normally start by establishing the position and shape of all of the full beams and then work forward and aft of these for the remaining deck structure. If the deck is to be flat and have no camber, then life is simple and your main complete beam just forward of the coachhouse can be positioned and simply housed into the inwales (Figure 72).

Establishing the camber curve and therefore the amount of curve for each beam is not too difficult once the camber curve has been established. Each boatyard would have a different way of drawing the camber curve – some quite complicated. The problem is, that as well as the width of beam changing as you go forward and aft on the hull, the sheer curve (side profile of the gunwale) changes too. Some builders have quite involved ways of dealing with this but, frankly, so long as you are willing to make small individual adjustments to the curve of the beams,

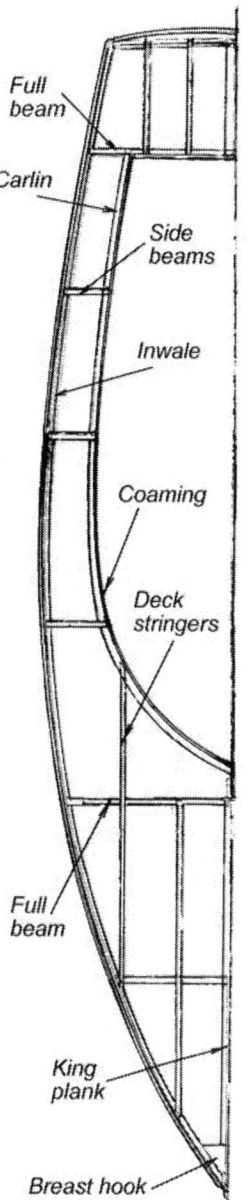

Fig 71. The deck structure layout for the Selway Fisher 6m Swift design.

judiciously using a plane, I stick with a fairly simple method.

First a plywood or scrap wood template is made of the full camber curve. The camber should be marked on the deck construction drawing. Typically for a 20' (6.10m) long boat it will be something like 2 3/4" (70mm in 7' (2.14m) of beam. This means that the maximum depth of the camber (the height of

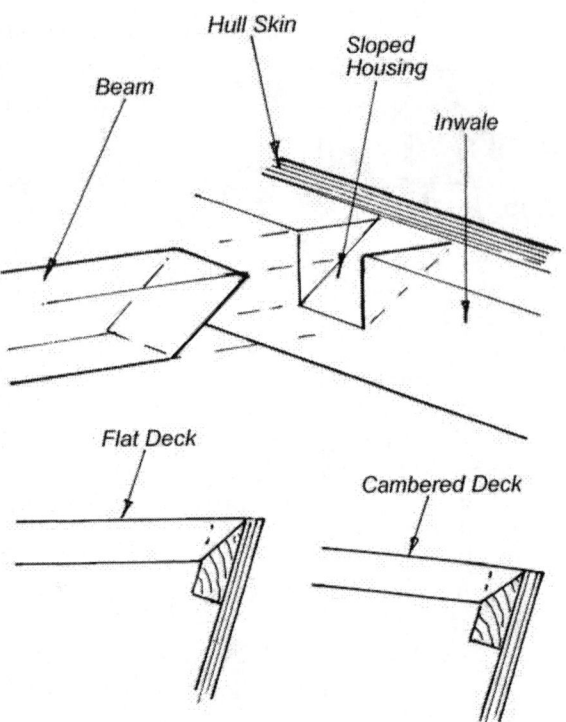

Fig 72. Fitting the deck beams to the inwale—note, most decked boats will not have hollow (open pattern) inwales.

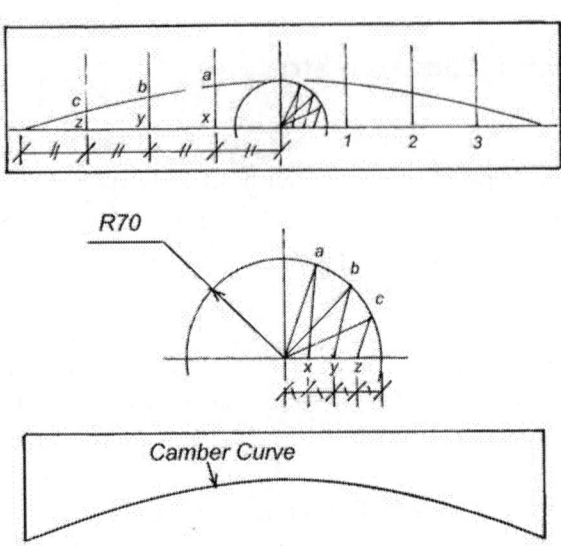

Fig 73. Drawing and cutting the camber curve.

the camber hill, so to speak) is 2 3/4" at a maximum hull beam of 7' – the actual beam of the boat may be slightly less than 7' but this does not matter. As the camber goes forward and the beam reduces, so the camber height reduces until right at the tip of the bow, where there is no beam, there is also no camber.

To make up the template for the camber curve draw a straight line on your template material and at it's centre point raise a perpendicular line. Where these two lines meet use this as the centre of a semi-circle with a radius equal to the maximum camber height. For the length of the horizontal line left and right of this centre mark off your 4' (1/2 beam) and divide these distances into 4 equal parts and raise perpendicular lines (1,2 and 3) at these points (Figure 73).

From the centre of the semi-circle draw lines at 45, 22 ½ and 67 ½ degrees to cut the circle at points a, b and c. Divide the horizontal radius of the circle into 4 equal parts marked x, y and z. the length of the lines x-a, y-b and z-c are then transferred to the lines 1.2 and 3 and the points joined up in a curve – do the same on the other side and you now have your complete camber curve. Finally, carefully cut this curve out preserving the top part which is now your camber template.

All you now do is rest this template across the gunwales at any point along the length of the hull and you have the curve and camber height at that point – it will give you the shape of any beam at whatever point you position the curve along the length of the boat (Figure 74).

The strongest and least wasteful way to make up a cambered deck beam is to laminate it – once the camber curve has been established for a particular beam, it can laminated in a number of ways. Here is just one method, where the curve is drawn down

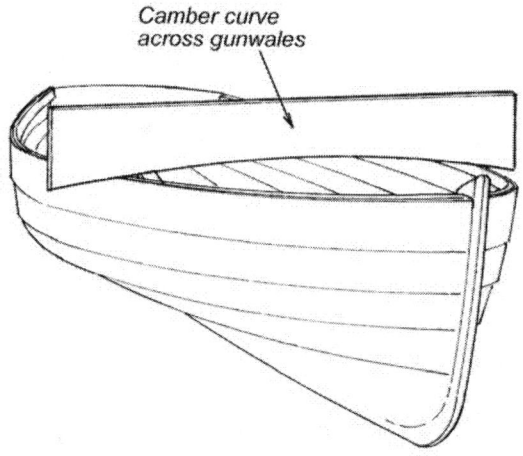

Fig 74. Using the camber curve across the gunwales.

onto thick chipboard base and the curve is defined by a series of steel angle brackets bolted to the base so that their faces lie perpendicularly from the curve. The wood laminates can then be clamped to these steel with glue between them whilst the glue cures (Figure 75).

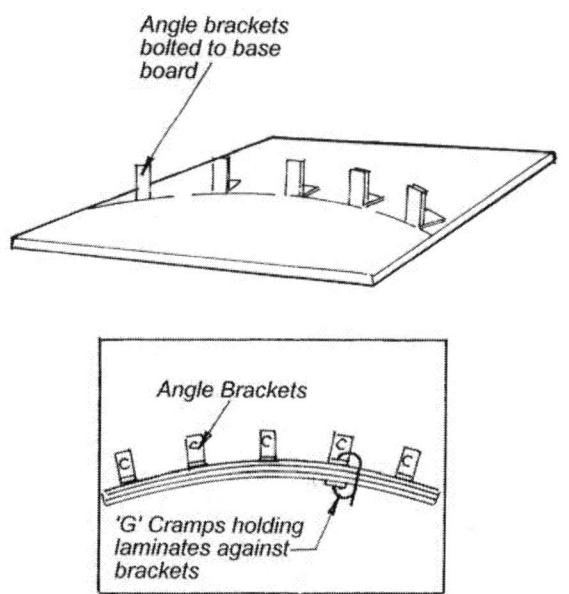

Fig 75. A jig for laminating the deck beams.

If the brackets are a foot (0.3m) or so tall, several beams can be laminated at the same time as the curve remains the same for most of the beams – it is just the width that changes. Once the beams have been laminated, they can be removed from the jig and cleaned up ready to have their ends shaped to fit the join into the inwale (Figure 76). For both cambered and un-cambered decks, it very important that the bottom of the cut and shaped end of the beams does not lie 'proud' (outside) of the inwale but is fully seated in the inwale—this would mean that the beam is unable to use all it's stiffness and strength to support the deck. Sometimes the end of the beam is housed further into the inwale with a horizontal 'landing' cut onto the bottom of the notch cut into the inwale. However, this may weaken the inwale more than necessary.

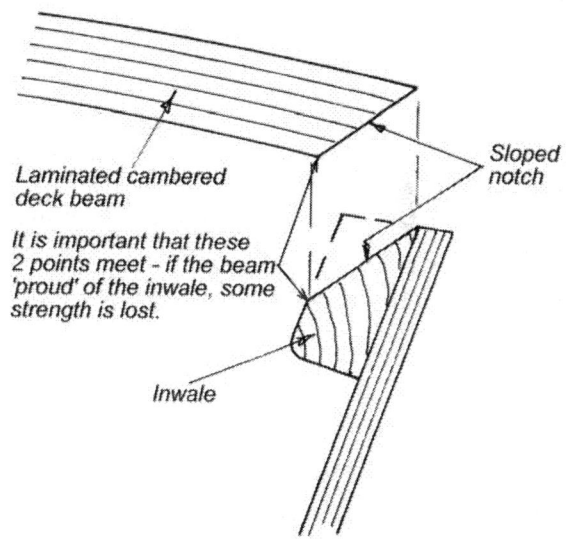

Fig 76. Fitting a laminated and cambered deck beam.

An alternative way to make cambered beams is simply to cut them from the solid plank but if they are shaped on their underside, this gives them short grain areas which are weak (Figure 77).

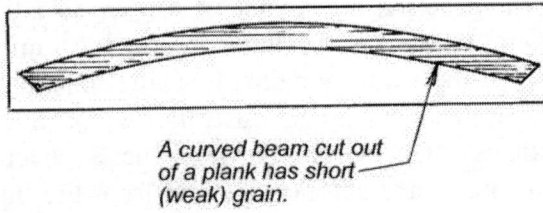

A curved beam cut out of a plank has short (weak) grain.

Fig 77. The weakness of cutting a curved beam from a plank.

If the beam is up against a bulkhead with no need to worry about the headroom of any opening through the bulkhead, then there is no reason why the bottom cannot be kept flat which avoids this problem and makes for an easily shaped beam (Figure 78).

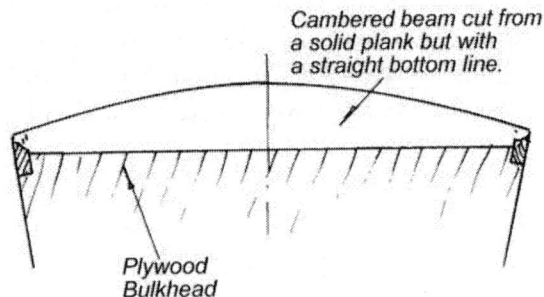

Cambered beam cut from a solid plank but with a straight bottom line.

Plywood Bulkhead

Fig 78. A curved and solid beam against a bulkhead.

If there are intermediate bulkheads running up under the side decks this makes it easier for establishing how the carlin runs and also for fixing it in place. If there are no intermediate bulkheads or frames, the carlin needs to be fixed in position using simple plywood clamps – the width of the side deck at various points should be given on the drawings (Figure 79).

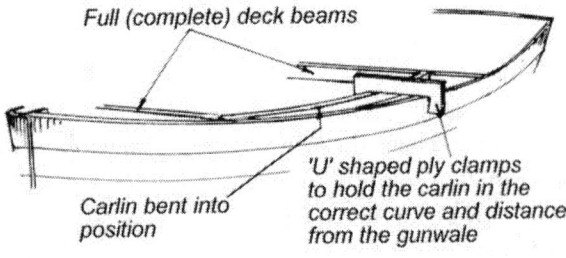

Full (complete) deck beams

'U' shaped ply clamps to hold the carlin in the correct curve and distance from the gunwale

Carlin bent into position

Fig 79. Ply clamps used to hold the carlin in place.

The carlins can then be laminated either permanently in place or, so that they can be more easily cleaned up on the bench, dry fitted to the beams.

King planks and under deck blocking such as the breast hook can now be fitted and any specific blocks used for particular deck fittings can also be fitted in place. The whole deck structure should then be faired and cleaned up. You may want to do any final sanding and even varnishing/painting of the deck structure now, before the deck itself goes on – it is much easier at this stage, but do keep paints etc off the top surface of the deck structure where it will be glued to the decking.

9.6.2 The Deck

We will assume that the deck itself is plywood. A plywood deck acts as a massive strength member by imparting to the plan-form shape of the boat, stiffness and stability in shape. Rather than having individual planks running fore and aft, we have a sheet stiffener and strength member tying all parts of the deck together in the horizontal plane.

The ply deck may go on in one thickness or in several thicknesses if there is a lot of camber. If the plywood is applied in several layers then joins in successive layers should be staggered – if not and only one thickness is applied, I like to use butt straps much like those for the hull planking. Of course, if there is blocking or framework under the deck, these can act as butt straps too. Some builders arrange joins in the plywood over the beams and 'snipe' the joins – this is good practice so long as there is a large enough glue area to prevent movement (Figure 80).

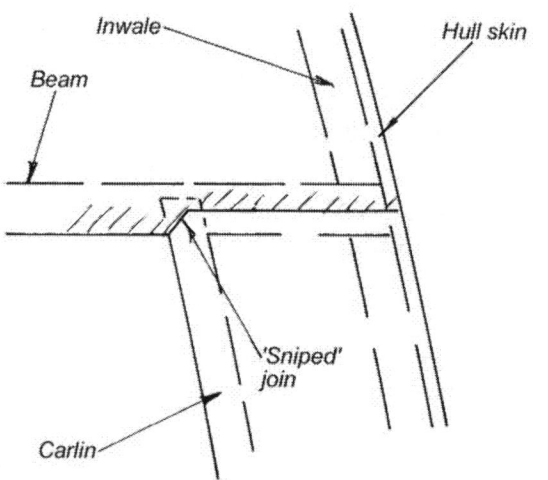

Fig 80. 'Sniped' joins over the beams.

Above—the curved deck beams and side decks being fitted to Ian Parsons Stornoway 14.

9.7 Coamings

Most dinghies and small dayboats will not have coamings on the inboard edge of side decks—they do help keep water out of the cockpit and increase the angle of heel before water enters the cockpit but they are uncomfortable if you want to sit on the side deck unless you have a seat unit made to sit on top of the coaming.

Because coamings often follow the fore and aft curvature of the deck they will either have to be cut out of a large plank or be laminated. If they have a lot of shape in them and perhaps come to a point at the front they will need to be laminated as well. Make up a scrap ply or hardboard template to get their shape from the boat. Corners are sometimes finger jointed or even have dove-tail joints—otherwise the side is allowed to run past the athwartships pieces at the front and back of the cockpit and a fillet is used for the join.

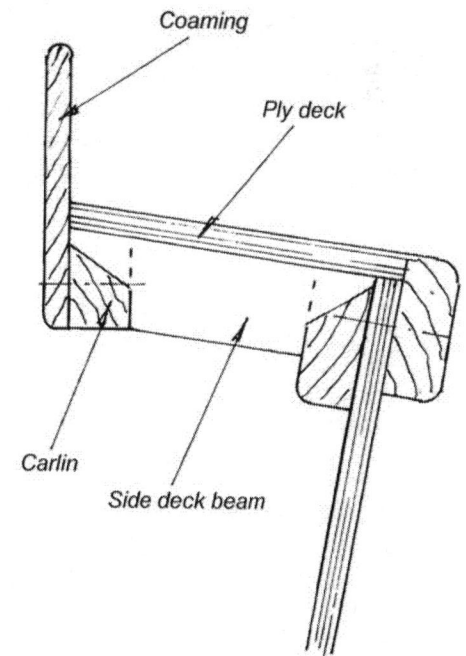

Fig 81. A typical coaming.

preferably of Yellow Pine. Make a simple ply or hardboard template of the area that is usefully to be covered by bottom boards and use this on the bench to sort out how your boards are best orientated. The boards are glued and screwed together and made up in easily removable sections (Figure 82). They may be kept in place with a simple turnbuckle arrangement.

For dinghies and dayboats they may also be made up out of 3/8" (9mm) plywood.

Above—the coaming is kept fairly low on this example of a Selway Fisher Chincoteague Skiff by Maddie Leach and is not too uncomfortable to sit on.

Above—the result of a comfortably fitted out 10'6" Northumbrian Coble!

9.8 Bottom Boards

Many dinghies do not bother with bottom boards but, although they add more weight, they are a good idea to keep the crew's weight off the hull bottom and to keep feet clear of bilge water.

I tend to make them up in an open pattern out of 3/8" x 3" (10x75mm) boards

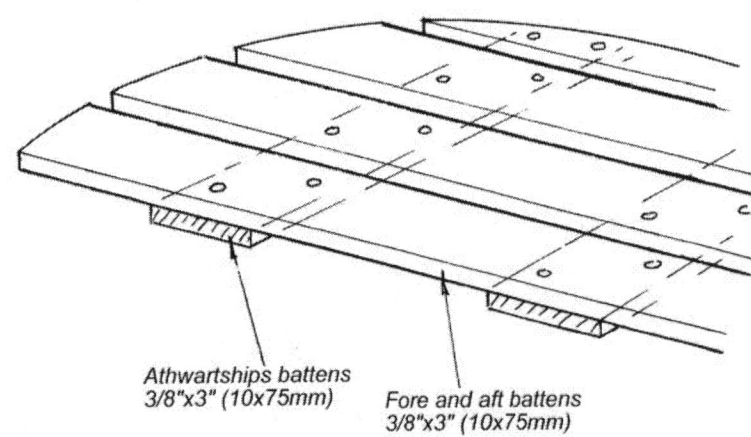

Athwartships battens
3/8"x3" (10x75mm)

Fore and aft battens
3/8"x3" (10x75mm)

Fig 82. Simple open pattern bottom boards.

Chapter 10
BUOYANCY (FLOTATION)

10.1 General

The term used when we look at keeping a boat afloat when it has been swamped either by being overwhelmed or by being involved in a collision, is *buoyancy*. More accurately, it should be called flotation. Buoyancy is really the force exerted on the boat, created by it's underwater volume (or the buoyant forces acting on the underwater part of the boat), which acts vertically upwards (to keep it afloat). But, most authorities and boating people use the term buoyancy and so we will stick to it here.

All wood boats, above the size of a simple dinghy, will sink when swamped because the amount of wood in them is not enough to support the weight of steel centreplates, outboard engine, rigging etc. Even a wood dinghy without all the metal weight will have insufficient natural buoyancy in it's wood structure to support the weight of a man when it has been swamped.

Let us first look at what buoyancy is supposed to provide :-

- It should provide enough 'lift' to a swamped boat, floating the boat high enough to support the crew in reasonable safety.
- It should facilitate 'righting' a capsized boat in such a way that when 'righted' the boat remains in a state of equilibrium and stability so that the boat is not in danger of capsizing again.
- Ideally, it should also provide sufficient 'lift' so that all openings (tops of transom/hull, centreboard case tops etc) are sufficiently above the swamped waterline such that the crew can bail

the boat out without having to have the boat towed ashore to do this.

In some boats, there is no point in trying to provide buoyancy to meet these criteria. As you move up in size to boats with large amounts of fixed ballast (including engine weights etc) or heavy bunkers (fuel in the form of coal for instance on steam launches), there is no point in trying to provide buoyancy because the volume required would allow no room for the crew!

I also think that it is dangerous to provide 'some' buoyancy when you could never provide enough to meet the requirements listed above—having inadequate buoyancy can lull the boat user into a state of false security.

10.2 Types of Buoyancy (Floatation)

For dinghies and dayboats there are three main types :-

- Fixed air chambers—these are tanks built into the structure of the boat usually under seats (thwarts), side benches and decks often sealed but sometimes with some form of water-tight hatch either for inspection or so that they can also be used for stowage. Such chambers are not, in the true sense, buoyancy chambers—if they are broached by collision, most of the buoyant 'lift' is lost. They can often leak without the crew knowing it and if they are filled with gear, they actually add to the sinking force. Filling them with sealed plastic containers helps but it is worth noting, that authorities like the US Coast Guard do not count them into their buoyancy requirements—they are excluded as inadequate.
- Foam filled chambers—these are

perhaps the same chambers mentioned above, but filled with a foam of closed cell type which will not soak up water (REP– Rigid Expanded Polyurethane Foam for instance) - such filled tanks are known as 'permanent' buoyancy.
- Buoyancy bags—these are purpose made bags of tough construction which are secured, often with straps, to the boat structure. Their advantage over air chambers is that you can immediately see whether they are damaged or not but securing them properly can be a problem.

One important note here—whatever buoyancy is fitted, it must be very securely attached to the hull. A small bag or chamber measuring just 1' x 2' x 2' (0.3x0.60x0.6m) will have a volume of 4 cubic feet (0.11 cubic metres) which will give approximately 250 lbs (113kg) of lift which is equivalent to 1/8th of a ton using a figure of 65 lbs/cu.ft (1040kg/cu.m)! Tying strong empty plastic bottles by their necks to a seat is not enough!

10.3 Disposition of Buoyancy (Flotation)

Apart from having adequate buoyancy we must also make sure that it is in the correct place. Too much buoyancy can be as bad as having too little—it can keep a small boat inverted not allowing you to right the boat if the buoyancy is fitted too low in the hull. If the boat has capsized but not inverted, too much buoyancy will make the boat float so high that it is difficult for the crew to use the centreboard to pull the boat upright again and will make the bottom of the hull, now exposed to the wind, act like a sail, moving the boat around when you want it to be steady and forcing the hull further over until it inverts.

Buoyancy which is fitted too high will not come into play until the boat is well swamped—you will get no 'lift' out of it until the boat is well sunk which may mean the centreboard case tops are immersed. If the top of your centreboard case is immersed when the boat is swamped, you will never be able to bail the water out (Figure 83 and 84).

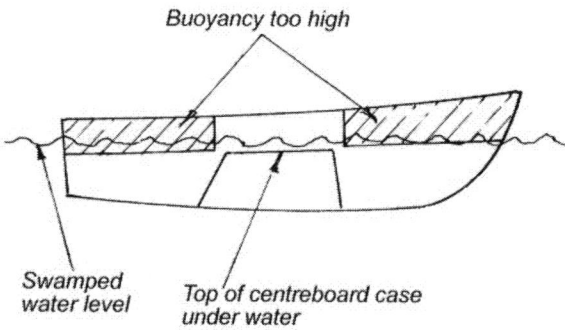

Fig 83. Buoyancy fitted too high.

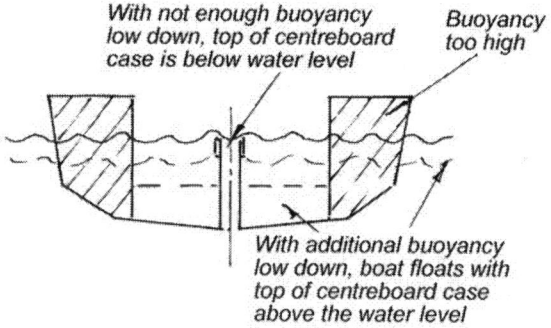

Fig 84. Buoyancy fitted too high—but fitting more lower down solves the problem.

If our boat normally carries an outboard motor this will always be in the wrong place when mounted, for level trim when swamped—the motor will pull the aft end down and unless more buoyancy is distributed aft to compensate for this, you may have a situation where the water is always slopping over the transom, not allowing you to bail the boat out (Figure 85).

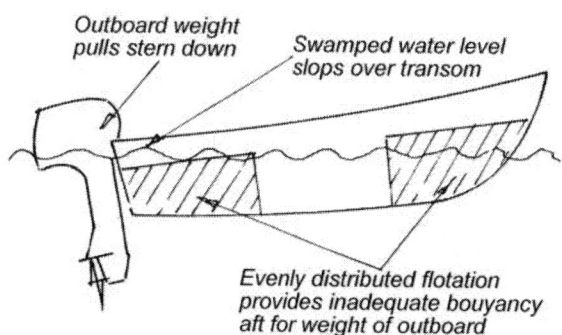

Fig 85. Wrongly positioned buoyancy—or not enough buoyancy aft.

Again, if buoyancy is fitted too low (which is what we want to keep the top of the centreboard case above water) the boat might float so high that it is difficult for the crew, who are exhausted and cold anyway, from getting back into the boat. On a sailing boat, buoyancy fitted too low will also act on the 'wrong' side of the boat's centre of gravity creating a capsizing force which will tend to invert the boat (Figure 86).

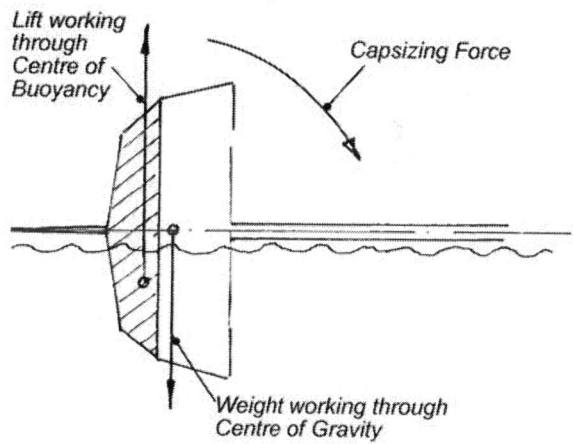

Fig 86. Buoyancy fitted so low on a sailing boat that it can create a further capsizing force sufficient to invert the boat.

If the buoyancy is distributed higher (Figure 87) the buoyant 'lift' force acts on the 'right' side of the Centre of Gravity, helping the boat to right itself.

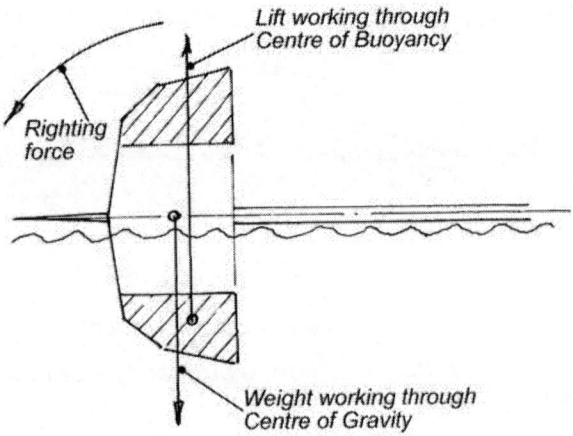

Fig 87. Buoyancy fitted higher which helps a sailing boat to right itself.

Overall, I like to have some permanent buoyancy in foam filled chambers adequate to at least keep the boat afloat with it's crew and then to have well fixed air bags which will allow you to make some adjustments to the disposition of some of the buoyancy. Do be warned though, bags may not be allowed under some regulations.

If you do have sealed air chambers do not have simple hatches with neoprene seals—use proper water-tight hatches from a manufacturer who properly makes and tests them.

10.4 How Much Buoyancy (Flotation) Do I Need?

A quick answer to this is to go for a figure equal to 2.5 times the total weight of the boat including outboard, gear etc in air. So, if your dinghy weighs 200 lbs (91 kgs) with a small outboard, the total buoyancy required will be approximately 500 lbs (228kg). How do I relate this to the volume of buoyancy required? Well, one cubic foot of salt water weighs 65lbs which means, in terms of buoyancy, one cubic foot of air immersed under water will give 65lbs of lift (one cubic

meter of air will give 1040kg of lift). So the volume required to give 500 lbs of lift will be 500 divided by 65 which equals 7.7 cubic feet. So, if we have 2.5 cubic feet aft, 2.5 cubic feet forward and 2.7 cubic feet under the centre thwart that is a good start. I would also add a further 20 lbs of lift (0.3 cubic feet) for each crew member too.

To find out how much buoyancy is required just to keep the boat afloat you can get an accurate figure by looking at the buoyancy requirements of each item on the boat and summing them all up. We will not get too scientific here but just point out that some materials are lighter than water and will naturally float—wood for instance and others are heavier than water and will sink—metals, glass fibre etc. but if we remember the experiments in the physics lab at school when we looked at Archimedes' work, we will remember that when an object is immersed in water it 'effectively weighs less' than it does in air. In other words, despite the fact that it sinks, the water does impart to it some lifting force. The amount of lifting force depends on the relative density of the material with metals getting less than fibreglass for instance, because the metal is more dense in relation to water than the fibreglass. It is by looking at the individual lifting forces on each material which goes to make up our boat, that we can decide on just how much buoyancy is required.

We must also remember in our calculations that whilst air effectively has no weight and gives 65 lbs of lift in salt water, the closed cell foam used in a foam filled chamber has some weight of it's own to support and therefore will only give around 60lbs of lift per cubic foot (960 kg per cubic metre).

The relative amount of lift we get for each different material is defined by it's

'Buoyancy factor' (Bb) which is simply calculated by taking a sample of the material and weighing it whilst submerged in water and then dividing this weight by it's weight in air. You do not need to worry about doing this for yourself because I give the Bb figures I use for the most common materials and items below—many are averages but good enough for our purposes and if you need more you can interpolate from the figures given.

Material/Item	Buoyancy Factor (Bb)
Glass Reinforced Plastic	0.33
Man	0.1
Aluminium	0.63
Steel	0.88
Lead	0.92
Softwoods (average)	-0.92
Hardwoods (average)	-0.39
Plywood (average)	-0.6
Foam	-61.5
Sail Cloth	0.09
Stores, water etc	0.5
Equipment (average)	0.5

Note that items in the above table that have negative Buoyancy factors do so because they contribute to the lift or buoyant force keeping the boat afloat. If we multiply the weight of each item on our boat by it's buoyancy factor we get a figure for the amount of buoyancy required.

On Page 70 we look at a couple of examples but remember, these calculations will only give the buoyancy required to just keep the boat afloat—*they are not what would be required to allow the boat to float high enough to be bailed out or easily righted— that figure may be 5 or 10 times more* .

The US Coast Guard and other official bodies have their own requirements and you must follow these when using your boat in waters under their jurisdiction—the above is only a first guide but, as already mentioned, I have found that a figure of 2.5 times the weight of the boat plus gear in air is a pretty good figure to work on.

Having calculated and fitted your buoyancy, have you got it right? There is only one way to find out and that is to choose a nice warm day, don your swimming costume plus life jacket and test your boat. Swamping is easy—just fill your boat with buckets of water but you will find it quite hard to actually capsize the boat. *Do not immerse the outboard etc* but use an equivalent weight positioned in the same place.

Having gone through this exercise, just remember that should you get swamped or capsize or hit a semi submerged object, it is likely that conditions will not be ideal. It will not be a flat calm on a sunny day!

10.5 A Note on Self Righting

Be careful, a truly self righting boat is a boat that is unstable in the inverted position such that it quickly recovers to an upright position if inverted. In practice, unless all hatches are sealed in the inverted position, there is sufficient fixed ballast low down and the boat haas plenty of volume in it's coachroof/deck shape, it is difficult to have a self righting boat.

Never trust literature or anybody who says that a boat is self righting without seeing evidence and remember that rig, sails, waves and wind make self righting very difficult. RNLI lifeboats are self righting because of the weight and shape of their hulls and the large volume of their superstructures which make them unstable in the inverted position.

A 12' Dinghy

Item	Material	Weight (W) (lbs/kg)	Buoyancy Factor (Bb)	Buoyancy Required W x Bb (lbs/kg)
Hull skin	Plywood	75/34	-0.6	-45/20
Hull framing etc	Douglas Fir etc	45/20	-0.92	-41/19
Outboard motor	Steel	200/91	0.88	176/80
2 x Crew	Man	400/181	0.1	40/18
Gear etc	Sails, fittings etc	60/27	0.75	45/20
Total buoyancy required to just keep the boat afloat				**175/79**

This is equivalent to 175/65 = 2.7 cubic feet or 0.077 cubic metres

A 16' Dayboat

Item	Material	Weight (W) (lbs/kg)	Buoyancy Factor (Bb)	Buoyancy Required W x Bb (lbs/kg)
Hull skin	Plywood	350/159	-0.6	-210/95
Hull framing etc	Douglas Fir etc	150/68	-0.92	-138/63
Outboard motor	Steel	240/109	0.88	211/96
Centreplate/ballast	Steel	250/113	0.88	220/99
4 x Crew	Man	800/363	0.1	80/36
Gear etc	Sails, fittings etc	150/68	0.75	113/51
Total buoyancy required to just keep the boat afloat				**276/124**

This is equivalent to 276/65 = 4.25 cubic feet or 0.121 cubic metres

Remember that the above figures are just to keep the boat afloat and not what would be required to help right or bail her out—that would need 5 to 10 times the above amount.

Chapter 11
SHEATHING, COATINGS & FINISHES

11.1 Sheathing

There are two reasons for sheathing your boat. The first, is to give the outside of the hull an abrasion resistant finish that will also act as a barrier to water and help prevent leaks. the second, is to add strength and stiffness to the hull and superstructure shell. The increase in strength, will be to both the impact resistance and to the tensile strength of the boat.

Just how much abrasion resistance, water proofing and strengthening that will occur, will depend on the materials that you use and on the efficient bonding between the wood boat and the sheathing.

Up in the Scottish yards, we used to use a nylon Cascover sheathing which was very efficient in all respects but was difficult to apply. The choice for the amateur comes down to glass based cloths in either polyester or epoxy resin.

There is no doubt that the latter, is by far the best, with excellent bonding qualities and increased strength to the boat structure, but it is expensive.

I have also sheathed with polyester resin and have, in the main, had success. However, with this material, which definitely does not bond to the wood as well as epoxy, you have to keep an eye out for the sheathing parting from the hull and repair such areas immediately before water is able to travel further between the sheathing and the hull.

Preparation, for either epoxy or polyester, is all important. You must make sure that there are no protrusions or wood fibres sticking up which will cause air bubbles and voids below the cloth. Fill all gaps with resin putty and remove all sharp corners around which, the cloth will not go (Figure 88).

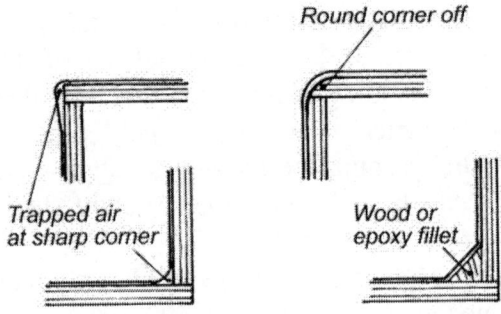

Fig 88. Preparing sharp changes in shape ready for sheathing.

When using polyester resin, I always lightly score the wood surface for a good mechanical bond (see 8.2) but without raising the wood fibre. Make sure that the surface to be sheathed is clean and free from all dust etc., and then prime with a coat of well catalysed resin. If you are using polyester resin, let this coat cure and then lightly sand to remove any protruding fibres before going onto the next stage.

If you are using epoxy resin, once the priming resin has been applied, if the surface looks dull and matt, then let it cure hard and sand as above. If however, the surface remains glossy, then you can apply the cloth straight onto the priming resin after it has only partially cured. If you have large voids to fill in the surface of the hull, let the resin cure and then fill with a resin putty before proceeding with the sheathing.

There are basically two methods for applying the cloth. The 'wet' and 'dry' methods. The 'wet' method requires that you apply resin to the wood surface first and then lay the cloth onto it rolling it down with split washer rollers. The problem here, is that you have to work fast in order to get the whole piece of cloth that you are working on, thoroughly wetted out before the resin starts to cure. This means having a team to help you. If you are working on vertical surfaces, this is really the only way to do it. If you are using epoxies, then use the slow hardener for the 'wet' method.

The 'dry' method entails holding the cloth into position with some tape, and then working resin into the cloth from above ensuring that it becomes well wetted out with no dry areas. This method is easier, in that, it allows you to work at your own pace without having to rush in order to wet the cloth out before all the previously applied resin cures but it cannot be used on vertical surfaces and you must ensure a thorough wetting out of the cloth and the removal of all air bubbles.

Work from the centre of the cloth in both cases using split washer rollers and squeegees (foam covered rollers). Do not over work an area especially with epoxy as this will tend to create bubbles in the resin.

Changes in shape in the surface being sheathed ie., from curve to flat will mean that the cloth will need to be cut as it is not possible to loose cloth by folding it. Consequently, darts will need to be cut out and the edges overlapped. Cloths are normally laid from keel to gunwale with a 2'' (50mm) overlap onto the other side of the hull (Figure 89). Adjacent cloths should also be overlapped where they meet, by approximately 1 1/2'' (36mm), and the lap well rolled down which will make it almost disappear. With epoxy resin, and if you are wanting to finish with an absolutely perfect

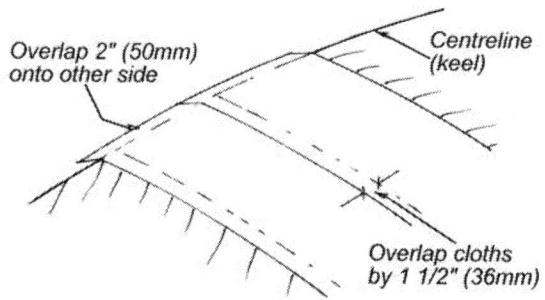

Fig 89. Typical overlaps in the sheathing.

surface which shows off the underlying wood grain, then the edges of the cloth can butt against each other leaving a flush surface. To do this, overlap the cloths slightly, and when the resin has partially cured, use a scalpel to cut a line through both cloths (Figure 90. The piece of cloth underneath can then be removed along with the excess piece on the top and the two cloths smoothed down exactly butting each other.

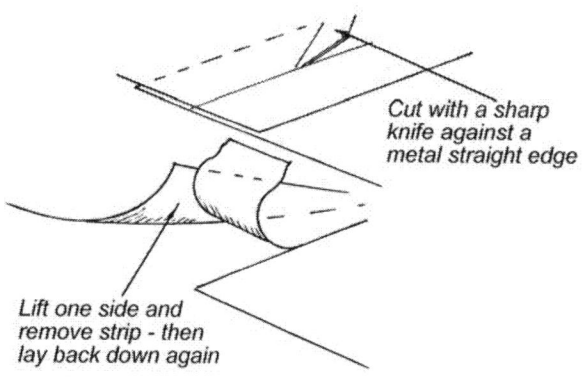

Fig 90. Cutting butts in the cloth.

At corners, cut the cloth diagonally and smooth down each piece of cloth. Then cut down the corner and remove the two excess pieces (Figure 91). Remember, try to avoid having sharp corners.

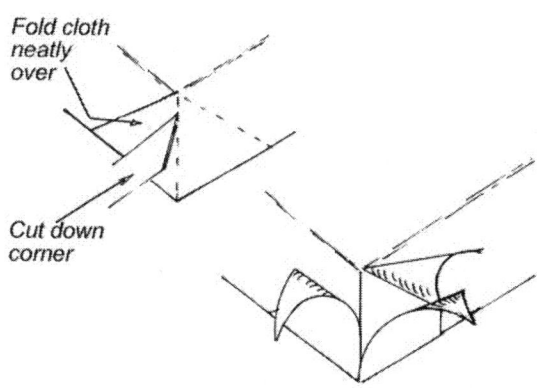

Fig 91. Sheathing around corners.

For boats up to 20' (6.1m) in length, I use a single layer of 8oz. per sq. yd. (280 gr.) woven roving. Before the resin has fully cured, I coat it with another layer of resin to fill the weave of the cloth. This coat, if it is polyester, and any others applied, can be pigmented with a colour paste.

For larger boats, or on small boats where the sheathing forms part of the stiffness of the boat you can use a layer of 1 1/2 oz. per sq. ft. (450 gr.) chopped strand mat followed by a layer of surface tissue although I have only ever done this with polyester resin. I would imagine that the thicker epoxy resin would not work very well with the surface tissue.

Although epoxy coated boats are sometimes sheathed on both sides of the hull especially where the sheathing is calculated as part of the strength of the boat, boats are usually only sheathed on their outside otherwise water entering the wood and trapped there will cause delamination and rot. Also, with polyester resin, as the resin cures, it contracts and on the outside of the hull where it is applied over a convex shape, the cloth grips the hull. The opposite to this would happen on the inside of the hull and the cloth would tend to pull away from the hull.

With this latter point in mind, if you have to sheath over any concave surfaces on the outside of the hull, for instance around propeller tunnels, then it is a good idea to use some form of metal or wood trim fastened over the sheathing to help keep it in place.

You should also sheath the hull before you fit runners and rubbing strakes etc., and fasten them over the sheathing so that they help to retain the sheathing (Figure 92). Bed the strakes in resin putty or a rubber adhesive. Sheathed decks can be made non slip by sprinkling Carborundum grit or fine sand onto the final coat of resin before it cures. Mask off areas that are to be kept free of the grit, coat with resin and sift an even coat of grit over it. Put on more than you think necessary and do not try to cut or drill through gritted areas later as it quickly dulls cutting edges.

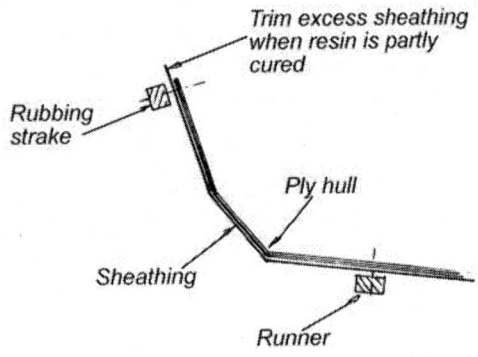

Fig 92. Fitting the strakes and rubbers after sheathing.

11.2 Coating with Epoxies

Coating the bare wood of your boat with epoxy resin will not significantly increase it's strength or even it's abrasion resistance (if using some of the thinner coatings), but it will provide an impervious barrier to water getting into the wood itself and increase it's life and there is no doubt that being able to say that your boat is epoxy coated does enhance it's resale value.

You can use general purpose epoxy resins to do the job although many boatbuilders find it too viscous (thick). There are several points to note when coating. First, make sure that all shaping and fairing of the wood surface is complete before you coat and make sure that the surface is absolutely clean and dry.

Filling small voids can be done after the surface has been coated and for a good varnish finish, a good well sanded surface is required using 120 grit sand paper.

If you coat hard surfaces such as metals, fibreglass or oak then use 80 grit sandpaper on them to provide a good mechanical key. On some metal surfaces a special primer should be used (contact the manufacturer). To gain good penetration with ordinary general purpose epoxies, the viscosity of the resin wants to be low and on cold surfaces pre warm the resin first before mixing in the hardener. Urethane foam rollers are best for an even application of the resin and you should not wait until a coat dries before you apply the next coat. Two coats are a minimum if you do not sand down between coats but if you sand to achieve a good finish, then 3 to 4 coats will be required. If using general purpose epoxies, the amount of resin used for coating will be quite high. Consequently, I tend to use some of the specially formulated coating resins. Examples are SP Systems Eposeal 300 with Ultravar 2000 varnish. Eposeal is very thin and can be applied with brush or rag and when you have got to the end of the boat you can go straight to the other end and start the next coat. Do use these products in a well ventilated area though.

Because they are thinner, more coats will be

required to gain a good depth of protection and I tend to use at least 5 coats if the resin is to be left uncovered by any other form of finish.

Another product from Structural Polymers is their SP320 Spacote which has been developed for laminating, coating and for structural filleting. It is thinner than ordinary general purpose epoxy resin and therefore easier to apply for coating but at the same time, it can be used for gluing and filleting making it a totally compatible system.

Make sure that the temperature of the wood has stabilised before you apply the resin so do not coat early in the morning or late afternoon when the ambient temperature will rise or fall. This is because the wood will release air from it's surface creating small bubbles in the resin (which can be brushed out). This is called 'out-gassing'. If a 'blush' (a waxy substance) occurs on the epoxy coated surface over night, wash it off with water using a light scouring pad. Dry the surface and lightly sand before applying the next coat.

11.3 Paint Finishes on Bare Wood

Keeping an eye on cost, I now rarely use Marine paint on small low cost boats which spend much of their time out of water. I do however, use a good Marine primer as a base ie., International Pink Primer and then use a good quality exterior house hold paint for the undercoat and topcoat. Again, on small boats, a good quality exterior household filler can be used to blend taped seams with the hull skin or to fill wood grain (see 11.3.2). On new wood, always use at least 1 coat of primer, 3 coats of undercoat and 2 coats of topcoat.

11.3.1 Preparing the Boat Prior to Painting

I have seen quite a number of boats which looked magnificent in their bare wood state, but which, when painted, looked terrible. Everyone is a painter - I mean that we have all painted the woodwork and walls in our house, and therefore we all think that we can produce a reasonable paint or varnish finish on our newly built boat.

We tend to forget that the woodwork in our new home is pre-finished or, has already been painted and therefore, all that is needed before attacking it with a paint brush, is a quick rub down with a fine sandpaper. Even plywood, unless it has a dense, high quality veneer on the outside, has a rough surface covered with rough wood fibres.

Consequently, your boat will need a lot of preparation before being painted or varnished. There are four important things to remember when finishing. The first is to use plenty of good lighting. You will never see whether a surface is ready for painting unless it is well illuminated. Virtually every yacht that I saw built during the time I worked in the boatyards, had plenty of blemishes in the paint and varnish work, once it had been moved from the building shed out onto the slip way prior to launching. Painting the boat outside using natural light is a good idea, but of course, dust picked up on a breeze can be a problem.

Linked to adequate light is the need to use your eyes. It sounds obvious, but spend time looking at the surfaces carefully hunting down roughness and blemishes in the wood finish.

Third, use your sense of touch and run your fingers over the wood surface. Sometimes, I have been able to pick up roughness easier using feel, than with the eye.

Lastly, plan the painting and varnishing sensibly so that you do not end up having to re-do areas because of paint splashes etc. Do all the sanding and preparation on all surfaces before starting any of the painting and varnishing. If you are going to paint and varnish adjacent areas, then complete the varnishing first and cut up to this with the paint and not the other way round. You can paint over varnish but you cannot varnish over paint. Similarly, paint light colours first and then paint up to them with darker colours.

Paint deck heads before lower areas so that any paint splashes will be covered. Similarly, paint or varnish the hull topsides before doing the boottop and bottom. On small painted dinghies and dayboats, a neat trick I have seen, is to define the waterline or boottop with a thin painted line. The easy way to do this, it to mark the rough position of the line on top of the undercoat and then to paint over this with the boottop colour in a fairly wide line. This paint line is allowed to dry/cure for several days and then the line is remarked onto the painted area. Masking tape of around 1" (25mm) is put on and carefully smoothed down along it's edges. Following this, the topsides and bottom can be painted and the masking tape finally removed to reveal a perfect paint strip. In doing this, be careful not to build up the paint thickness too much over the tape or you will rip paint off when removing the tape. Also, do not leave the tape on too long or it will stick fast to the original paint line and some of the paint line will come off on the underside of the tape.

Going back a stage to sanding, this is a crucial part of the finishing. The more time spent sanding, the better the final finish. For very rough timber (not plywood) start by using a course grain sand paper across the wood grain, to flatten it down. Only do this, on rough unplanned timber or where you have a deep blemish to remove.

Using the same grade of sand paper, sand at 90 degrees to the original direction, ie., with the grain, until you have removed all the marks made by the first sanding. Follow this by using a medium grade paper sanding with the drain to remove the marks left by the course sand paper. Finally, use smooth sand or cabinet paper to remove the marks left by the medium paper. Special attention needs to be spent on areas which will be varnished, especially in making sure that there are no sanding marks going across the grain - there is nothing which looks worse.

Having meticulously sanded the wood surfaces, get rid of all dust and debris by vacuuming and dusting. I do not like to wash down with white spirit, because this tends to raise the wood grain again.

As far as painting is concerned, my old woodwork master always said that it was better to use plenty of thin coats, rather than a few thick coats. I know that there are all sorts of 'one coat' paints on the household market, but I still prefer a paint which 1 can thin down so that I can put on several coats. When using conventional varnishes, the first coat is usually thinned so that it soaks well into the wood and I often apply a couple of coats of varnish and allow these to thoroughly dry before sanding (in other words I do not sand down after the first coat). When the first coats of paint or varnish dry, all the surface wood fibres become encapsulated within the coating so that they can be easily removed with the first light sanding.

There after, sand lightly between the coats

and remove the dust and debris carefully. I prefer to use Wet and Dry (or waterproof paper) paper for this as I find that it gives a much better finish. The problem in using this paper with water is that it is difficult to see when you are cutting back too far and sanding right through the coating and back into the wood.

Using a brush correctly is a bit of an art in itself. The trick is to coat the wood surface with sufficient paint or varnish without leaving 'holidays' (areas of no paint or varnish) or runs, with as few brush strokes as possible. There is little that can be said about this, because the technique you use will depend upon the paint or varnish that you use and how well it spreads onto the wood.

The old tried and trusted method of applying the coating in cross strokes which are then finished off with the brush stroke in one direction will sometimes leave brush marks when the paint or varnish dries. As a tip, I always find 'fiddling' around with the coat after it has been applied, to remove that r......y fly etc is a big mistake. You always end up making a small problem much bigger. In the end, if the final coat is a disaster, it will need to be cut back and re-coated - unless you can make an attractive feature of the problem area!

As far as the type of paint and varnish to use is concerned, there are so many different systems to choose from. If you are going to use an exterior household product for a dinghy or canoe, then use one from a manufacturer which you have used and got on well with, before. If you are painting over an epoxy coat, you must think about compatibility (see Chapter 8). I have not met many problems when using most house-hold paints except some of the single part polyurethane paints and varnishes. If in

doubt, consult the epoxy manufacturer.

There is no doubt that in a marine environment, a good quality yacht paint or varnish is well worth the cost if you want a long lasting, tough finish. You must decide whether the cost and effort put into your project so far, warrants the additional cost of marine finishes. My own rule of thumb, is that, if the boat is basically for knock-about use where you do not want to worry about scratches and general abuse showing, then use a good quality exterior household product. This is also true if the boat is going to spend most of it's time in the garage or upside down in the back garden. If, on the other hand, you have put plenty of good quality materials into the boat and you are going to worry about it's use and abuse, then compliment your craftsmanship with good marine paints and varnishes.

11.3.2 Eliminating the Bump Caused by Tapes on the Outside of the Hull

Even if you have not sunk or set the outside chine seam tape into a routed area (see 8.3.1.2) you can still achieve a perfect flat finish on the outside of the hull. It comes down to elbow grease and the careful application of fillers. First, make sure that the resin on the chine tapes is absolutely cured by leaving it a good 7 to 10 days before using a palm sander on it with 80 grit paper. Be careful not to go through the tape but use the sander to smooth the bump created by the tape, down and removing any hard edges.

Next apply a low density epoxy filler such as WEST 407 with a wide knife. Allow this to cure hard before using your palm sander again with the 80 grit paper. Repeat this process again if you wish.

Following this initial filling process, I wait

several days to let the filler properly cure and then start the paint process. Once the primer coat has dried I use a good quality exterior household filler again applied with a wide knife. I have used 'Everbuild All Purpose Ready Mixed Filler' which I find much tougher than other more well known brands of exterior filler. I use this between the undercoats and by the time I have got to the gloss painting stage I find that the tape bumps have more or less disappeared.

11.3.3 Striking the Waterline or Boottop

A simple way to strike a boot top line onto the hull, is to level the boat up on a hard level floor and then to attach a felt tip pen to the top of a piece of wood of the required height so that with the end of the wood resting on the floor and with the wood vertical, the pen can be used to spot a line on the hull at different points around the boat (Figure 93).

These spots can then be joined up with masking tape. You can alter the inclination of the boat by using chocks to make the boot top line deeper at the bow. Measure between the spots and a chine line on both sides at exactly the same point along the hull to make sure that you are marking the line level between the 2 sides.

Another method is to use a plastic tube with coloured water. Having marked the waterline, say at the bow, you simply need to get yourself a long clear plastic tube (the type used in fish tanks), fill it with water with a little dye in it and bend this into a 'U' so that you have both ends vertical. The level of the coloured water in both ends of the tube will be exactly the same. If you put one end of the

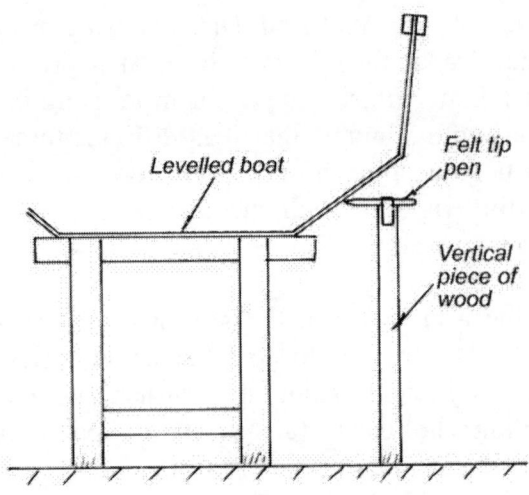

Fig 93. If you have a flat building floor you can use a simple post to help mark the waterline.

tube up against the mark for the waterline at the bow so that the water level corresponds with that of the waterline mark, wherever you take the other end of the tube along the hull, the level of coloured water in this remote end will also exactly correspond with the waterline mark (Figure 94).

Use this to mark more spots on the hull for the water line which you can then join up to mark the line right round the hull. A modern laser level set up on level platforms is also another easy way to mark the waterline on the hull.

Fig 94. Using a simple tube filled with coloured water to mark the waterline around the hull.

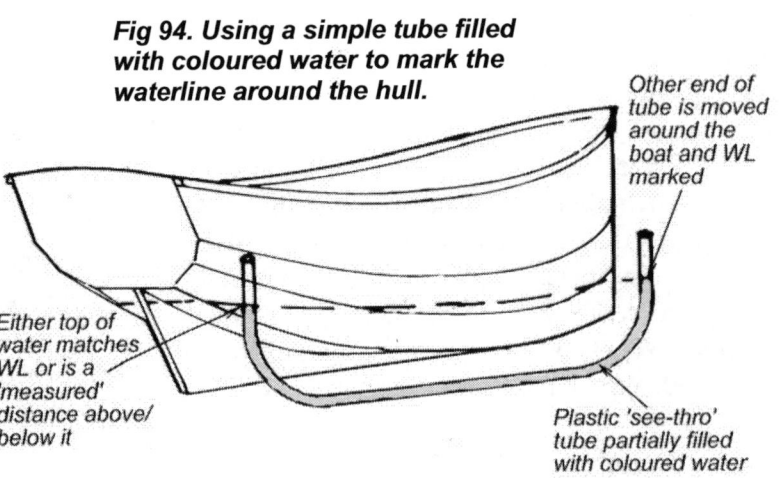

11.4 Safety

Boatbuilding using modern materials is fun and you can end up with a craft to be proud of very quickly and without the need for traditional boat building skills and tools. But, when dealing with modern glues and chemicals, it is sensible to take simple precautions for your own immediate and future protection.

This means taking the time to take care of your health. Don't go using modern materials without proper preparation and protection. Even when working on a small boat, there are some simple rules that will avoid problems later on :

1.   As far as possible, avoid direct skin contact with resins, hardeners and solvents (especially the latter two). I'm afraid that I tend to use a digit as an excellent application tool in areas where it is too difficult to use a spatula or brush, but if you do this, use disposable gloves.

2.   Do not use solvents to remove resin from your skin - use a resin removing cream (I have found Swafega excellent). Use a barrier cream for your hands when using a lot of resin.

3.   If there is a lot of resin splash and also when grinding cured resins, always use protective goggles or if you find these steam up too much, use protective glasses.

4.   The most important safety measure, is to use a dust mask when grinding and sanding, especially with cured resins and also when pouring and mixing some of the resin fillers. I hate using Colloidal Silica because it is very fine and lays on the chest. When mixing this substance, microfibres and microspheres, always where a mask.

5.   Be aware of fire hazards. Many of the materials are flammable and also epoxy curing in a pot will produce quite a lot of heat.

Finally, some people are or can become sensitive to various materials. After many years in intimate contact with epoxies I have never suffered health problems with them. I did have problems many years ago when I used some Cascamite (which is not an epoxy) because I allowed it to dry on my hands and my skin suffered! However, I have heard of some people having problems with epoxy sometimes with an allergic skin rash. This may be more to do with the wood than the epoxy - some people have a sensitivity to some types of fine wood dust. But in any case, do take sensible precautions and if you do have problems, contact the resin manufacturer.

On this page a further three views of a 15' Northumbrian Coble being built by Sam Hotchins during the fit-out stage. Note that the centreboard case cuts one of the frames and butts against another—in this case the frames were fitted before the case.

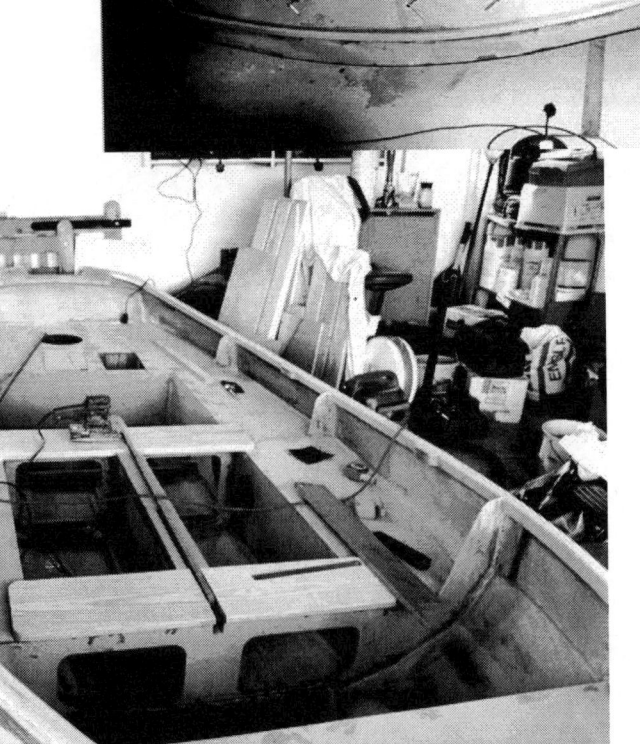

Chapter 12

MASTS AND SPARS
SOLID AND HOLLOW

12.1 General Notes

There are many different ways to make up masts and spars in wood depending on whether you are going to make them solid or hollow or round, pear-shaped, elliptical or box shaped.

Several books, go into the various different ways of constructing masts and spars. In this manual, I shall look at the most common methods used along with pointers towards some of the skills and methods required.

12.2 Materials for Wood Masts and Spars

Clear and quarter sawn Silver or Sitka Spruce is the best wood to use – it is light in weight - around 28 lbs/cu.ft (450 kg/cu.m), relatively stiff and strong and easily glued. This makes it ideal for a part of your boat that you want to be light in weight whilst at the same time, strong. But Sitka Spruce is not so easily available in clear long lengths today. Clear British Columbian Pine is a reasonable substitute, along with Douglas Fir. The problem I find, with Douglas Fir, apart from it's greater weight (33 lbs/cu.ft – 530 kg/cu.m), is that it's density can vary quite a lot within a board length.

I have seen some masts where Douglas Fir has been substituted for Sitka Spruce using the same dimensions for the mast diameter. The boat has been over powered by the additional weight of dense Douglas Fir aloft, making the boat very un-stable. For most hollow masts and spars, if Douglas Fir is used instead of Sitka Spruce the thickness of the staves used to make up the spar can be reduced proportionally with the different densities, so long as the gluing surfaces are not reduced significantly and the outside diameters of the spar are not altered. In other words, the thickness of a stave can be reduced by a factor of 28/33 = 0.85.

When laying out the staves for a solid or hollow mast or spar, do so in a way that reduces any tendency to warp. This generally means that adjacent pieces of wood are glued together with opposing grain – Figure 95.

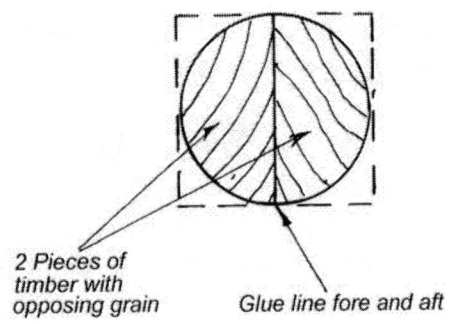

2 Pieces of timber with opposing grain

Glue line fore and aft

Fig 95. Making a solid mast from two pieces of wood glued with opposing grain to help prevent warp.

12.3 Solid Masts and Spars

Even if, for a small boat, you are able to obtain a piece of wood that has enough thickness to cater for the widest diameter of the mast/spar required, it is good practice to glue up the wood from at least two pieces (Figure 116). With a solid piece of wood, you do not know quite what shape it might warp or twist into later. By deliberately making up the mast/spar from at least two pieces with opposing grain, you are building into it, an anti- warping construction. Also, with a solid

piece of timber, it is more difficult to guarantee that the centre of the timber is free of faults – sap pockets, shakes (splits) etc.

The most basic details on a boat design should include dimensions for the diameter (or width and thickness for a square spar) at various points along the length of the mast/spar. Having glued up the wood to form the solid spar to the maximum width/depth specified, the next step is to draw out the spars tapers onto the wood.

We will take for example, a mast with a length of 20' (6.10m) with diameters of 2 1/4" (57mm) at the heel, 3" (76mm) a further 3' (0.92m) up at the partners, 2 1/2" (64mm) another 12' (3.66m) up at the lower rigging point (hounds) and 1 5/8" (41mm) at the truck (top). To get the profile shape along the mast, we can simply take the piece of wood we have glued together, mark these diameters (maximum widths – or 'node' points) at the various points along the length and start planning between them. However, the tapers should not be straight lines between these four points - the profile shape should gradually change (Figure 96).

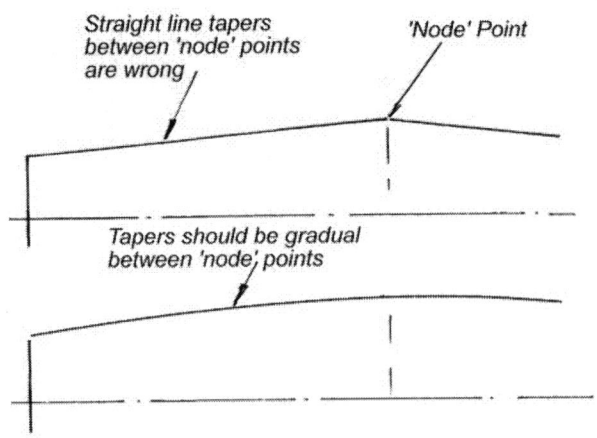

Straight line tapers between 'node' points are wrong

'Node' Point

Tapers should be gradual between 'node' points

Fig 96. Tapers on mast and spars should be gradual.

We achieve this 'smooth' transition between one diameter point (node) and another by plotting out the diameters at various other points between these nodes.

Figure 97 shows the section through the centreline of our mast with the node points (heel, partners, hounds and truck) marked on with their respective diameters. What we want to know is the diameters between these points for a smooth transition of the outside shape of the mast from one point to another.

and using the same radius, draw an arc who's centre is at 'B' to cut the horizontal line at 'C'.

Draw a line from 'B' to 'C'. Now, let us say that we want to define the diameters of the taper between the heel and the partners at three other, equally spaced points (d-e, f-g, h-i) – Figure 98

All we do now is to divide the base line between 'C' and the perpendicular into three equal parts (marked d, f and h) and do the

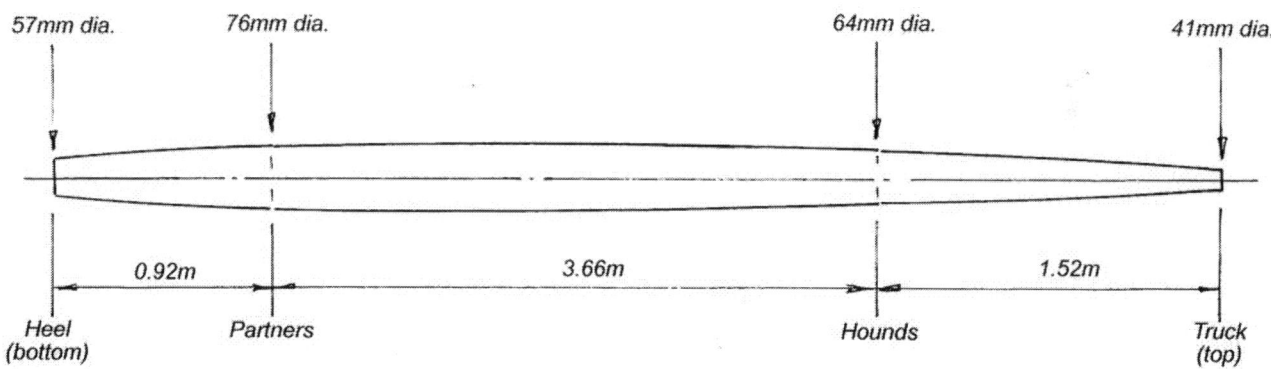

Fig 97. The layout of diameters on our example.

First, take a piece of paper, draw a horizontal base line and a perpendicular to it. Then, using the radius of the largest section through the mast (usually at the base or partners), use a compass to draw in a semi-circle – Figure 119 – in our example it will be a half of 3" (76mm) which is 1 ½" (38mm).

Let us first look at the portion of mast between the partners and the heel – using the compass draw in an arc who's centre is at one extreme of the previous semi-circle – point 'A', and who's radius is equal to that of the heel radius – in our case a half of 2 1/4" (57mm) which is 1 1/8" (28.5mm) to cut the first arc at point 'B'. Now take the compass

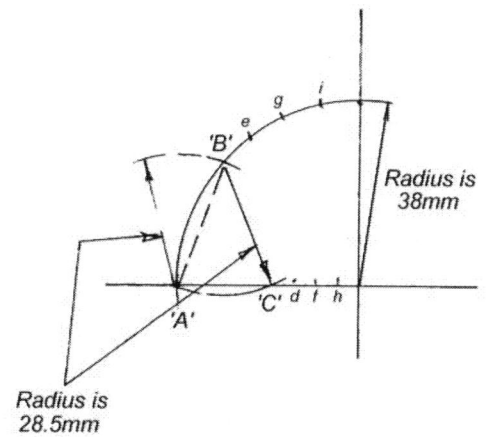

Fig 98. Starting to determine the diameters between 2 'node' points for a gradual taper.

same with the portion of the main arc from 'B' to where it is crossed by the perpendicular (marked e, g and i). Lines drawn between these points d-e, f-g and h-i now have lengths equal to the radii at these points. We can now divide up the portion of the mast between the heel and partners into 4 equal parts and mark these radii as half widths at the appropriate points (Figure 99).

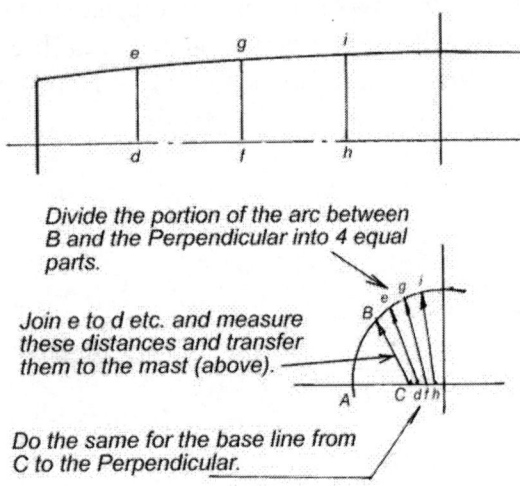

Fig 99. **Dividing portions of the main arc and base into equal divisions to gain the lengths of radii between 'node' points.**

The same process is used for the portion of the mast between the partners and the hounds. For the portion between the hounds and the truck we start afresh with a new main arc with a radius equal to that at the hounds.

If we take a long thin batten of wood and flex it to so that it's edge passes through all these points, we will have a fair and continuous curve from top to bottom. Mark this curve for the other side of the centreline – turn the wood over and do the same for opposite face. Clamp your wood securely and hew, cut and plane two of the faces carefully to these lines. Rotate the wood through 90

degrees and use the same dimensions to mark the 2 faces that have just been planed and hew, cut and plane the remaining two faces to these lines (Figure 100).

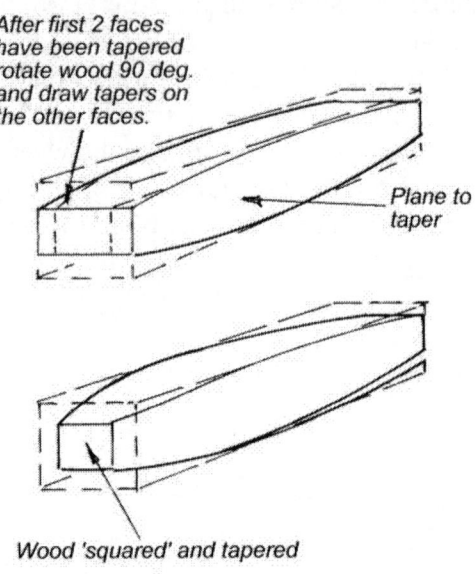

Fig 100. **Tapering the mast or spar once the tapers have been determined and marked out.**

You now have a piece of wood with square cross section and tapering as it should, from top to bottom. The next stage is to make it round and we do this by first, planing our wood into an eight sided shape. To mark the corners of the eight sided shape we use an "Eight–siding Gauge" which is simple enough to make up.

First, on a piece of paper, draw a full-size square to represent the mast or spars maximum section – in our case, a square with sides measuring 3" (76mm). Next, draw in the diagonals from corner to corner. Now use a compass with it's centre on one of the corners and with a radius equal to half the length of a diagonal, strike in an arc – do the same with the other corners – Figure 101.

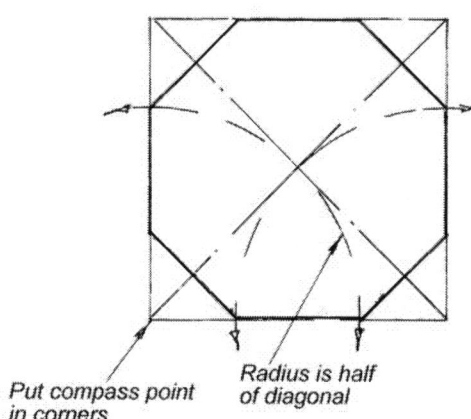

Fig 101. Drawing an 8 sided figure onto one end of the mast/spar.

Where the arcs cut the sides of the wood draw in lines to connect each adjacent pair and you now have an eight sided figure.

We can use this to make up our "Eight-siding Gauge". The gauge simply consists of a strip of wood with two nails pushed through it which are separated by a distance equal to the maximum width of the mast/spar (3" (76mm) in our case) and two other nails or two pencils set up to strike the corners of our eight sided figure – Figure 102.

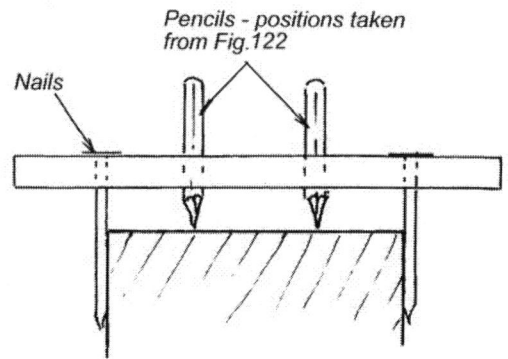

Fig 102. The 'Eight Siding Gauge'.

We simply slide this gauge along the mast/spar on each face making sure that the two outer guide nails remain against the faces of the wood at all times – this means that as the wood narrows due to the taper we have planed onto it, the gauge should swivel, tapering our corner lines automatically – Figure 103.

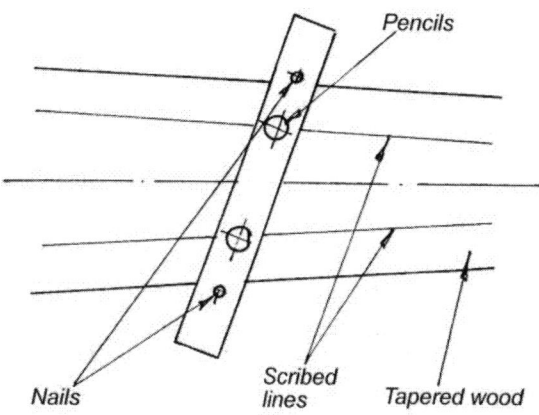

Fig 103. Using the 'Eight Siding Gauge' on a tapering mast/spar.

Of course, if the mast/spar is tapered in one direction only (with the maximum diameter at one end), you can mark the eight sided figure onto the largest end and set the gauge up to suit this without drawing it down onto paper.

You need to set saw horses up or a long bench, to support the wood on it's corners and plane each corner into a face. With the wood planed into it's eight sided shape you can now plane it up using a long bedded plane to 'knock off' the remaining eight corners and make it into a round shape. Finish with sandpaper. This last planning and then sanding should be done in a 'spiral' manner rather than simply planning up and down the length of the mast/spar. The main objective is not to over plane or sand and produce an oval rather than a round shape.

12.4 Hollow Masts and Spars

There are a number of ways to make up hollow masts and spars which can be divided into those that give 'box' or 'rectangular' sections and those which give round or oval/elliptical sections.

12.4.1 Round Section Hollow Masts and Spars

The simplest way to make up a hollow round mast or spar is to make up the length from two pieces of wood glued back to back as with the solid equivalent, and to hollow out a groove in each piece before gluing them together – this is very wasteful and easier to do on a parallel sectioned mast or spar. The inner and outer circles are first marked onto the ends of the timber and saw cuts made with a circular saw along the length of the groove. The remaining wood is then chiselled out. This process is more problematic for a tapered mast/spar where you want to keep constant wall thickness – you have to cut and chisel out the wood for the minimum internal diameter first and then adjust this carefully where more material needs to be removed. In the end, it is probably better just to cut out what is required for the smallest diameter throughout the mast/spar – Figure 104. If you are determined to go for a tapered hollow section, you can plane up the outside first and then make up a gauge similar to the "Eight-siding Gauge" to mark it out on the inside faces.

There are other methods of producing a hollow round spar from strips or staves of wood including the "Bird's Mouth" method, "Friendly Hexagonal" method and Cedar Strip method. There are good descriptions of these methods available in books, magazines and on the web – some are good only for round masts/spars, others can be used for

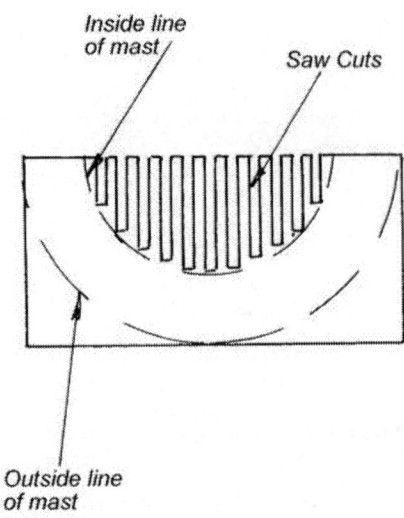

Fig 104. Hollowing out a mast/spar from solid wood.

elliptical shapes and most can be used for tapered masts and spars. Figure 105 shows some examples.

The Bird's Mouth method is interesting as the staves seem to be fairly easily machined. The diagram of a "Bird's Mouth" hollow mast shown in Figure 105 has eight pieces of wood "A" wide are used with a "bird's mouth" cut into one of each piece by cutting on a 45 degree angle deep enough to reach the centreline of the piece of wood. The finished mast/spar is 2.5 times the width of each individual piece and the thickness of each piece is half of it's width.

Most hollow masts and spars need solid pieces of wood in part of their hollow areas to take spreaders, mast bands etc – these along with the wood staves should be carefully assembled dry before gluing, to check that everything fits snug together. The solid inserts (cores) may have holes drilled through them to take wiring and halyards. The mast/spar must be carefully supported as it is

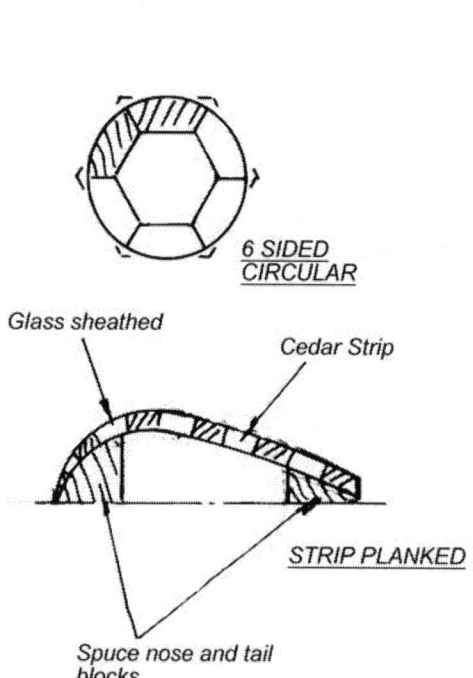

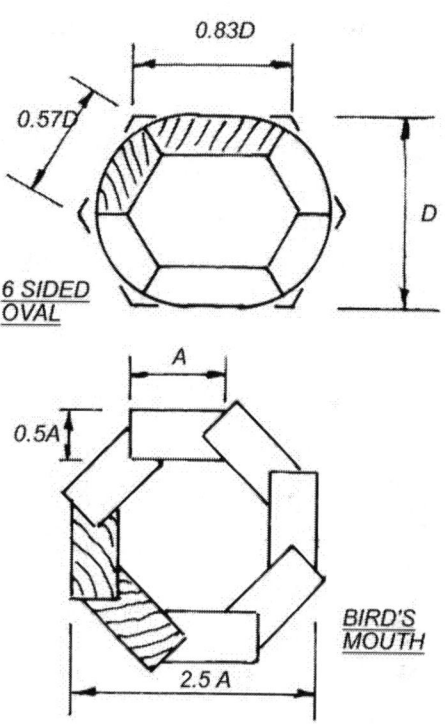

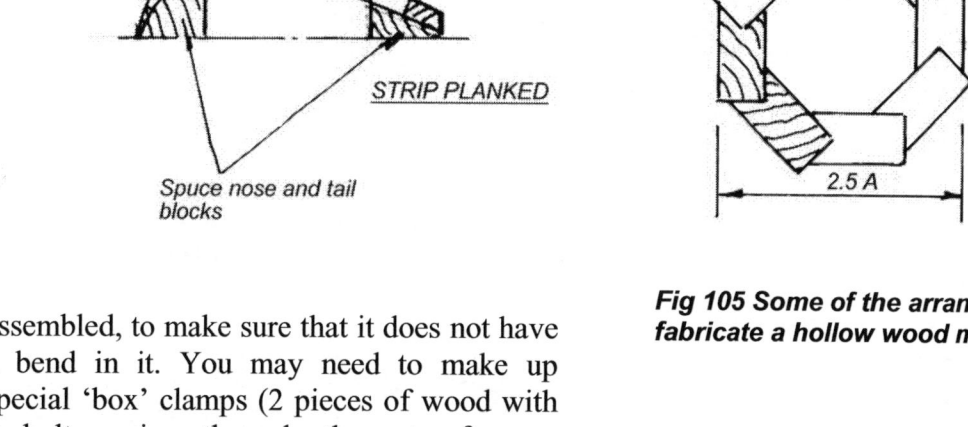

Fig 105 Some of the arrangements used to fabricate a hollow wood mast/spar.

assembled, to make sure that it does not have a bend in it. You may need to make up special 'box' clamps (2 pieces of wood with 2 bolts going through them to form a rectangle that can be tightened by tightening the bolts) to hold it all together – cable ties are also useful.

In the case of a strip planked mast, a greased 'mandrill' (a solid piece of wood shaped to the inside shape of the mast/spar) is sometimes used to clamp all the strips against to obtain the correct sectional shape – this is withdrawn once the glue has cured.

12.4.2 Rectangular Section Hollow Masts and Spars

Figure 106 gives some typical examples. If they are tapered, the tapered sides are marked out in much the same way as shown in Figures 97, 98 and 99. Support for the mast/spar during gluing is essential along

coloured glue line. Now of course you can use better glues such as epoxies or a polyurethane glue like Balcotan which cure without leaving a dark glue line. Aerodux 306 is still an excellent glue to use as well.

Fig 106—below. Examples of the arrangements of hollow box section mast/spars.

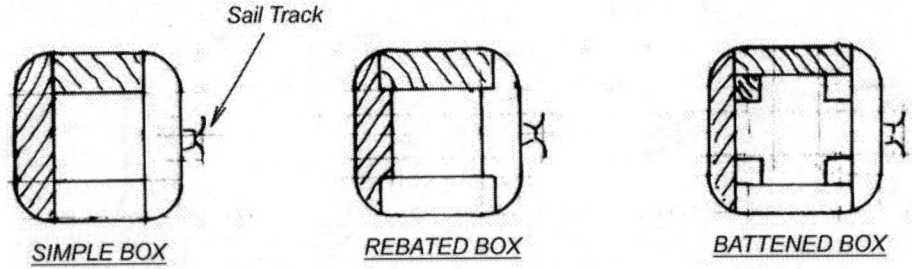

SIMPLE BOX   REBATED BOX   BATTENED BOX

Fig 107—below. The arrangement of 'inserts' in a hollow mast/spar for the various fittings.

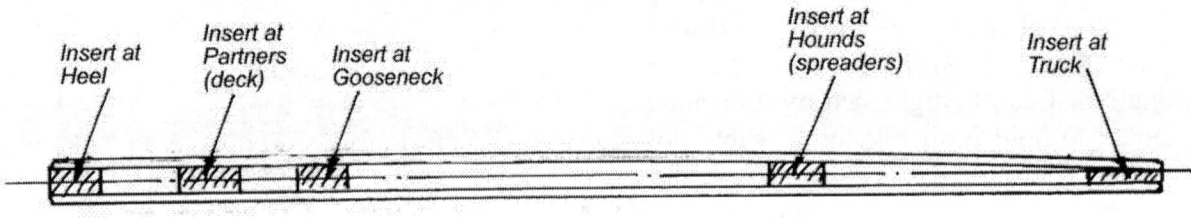

Insert at Heel — Insert at Partners (deck) — Insert at Gooseneck — Insert at Hounds (spreaders) — Insert at Truck

with firm and well spread clamping. Simple box clamps (Figure 108) can be used to help and this is definitely a case of 'the more, the merrier' - do not try to glue up a mast or spar with a minimum number of suitable clamps. Remember, there are few if any mechanical fastenings used in this exercise and the glue joins are therefore critical.

As far as glue is concerned, in the Yards pre-the 80's, we used glues like Cascamite (Extramite) or better still, Aerodux 306 because these glues dried with a clear or light

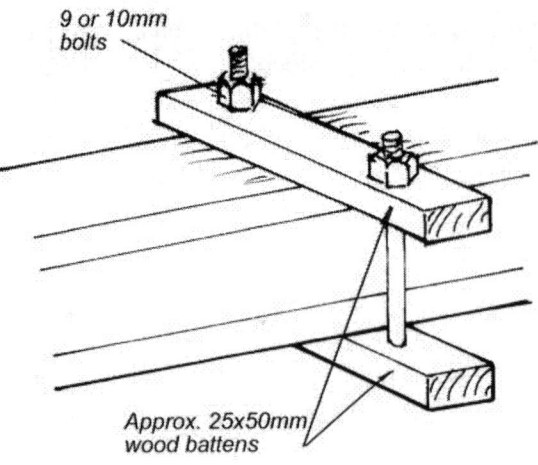

9 or 10mm bolts

Approx. 25x50mm wood battens

Fig 108. Box clamps are useful when gluing up a mast/spar.

Chapter 13

APPENDICES

13.1 Skegs & Keels

13.1.1 For Dinghies & Small Dayboats

Skegs and keels for small craft can be made up from gluing several layers of scrap plywood together to give the required thickness or they may be cut from solid wood. Many small plywood dinghies do not have a hog (inner keel) and in this case the skeg/keel will need to have a wood or epoxy fillet each side against the hull (Figure 109). Do make sure that all ply edge grain is covered or filled with thickened epoxy.

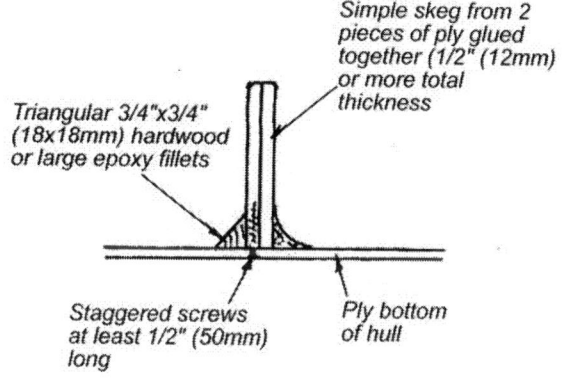

Simple skeg from 2 pieces of ply glued together (1/2" (12mm) or more total thickness

Triangular 3/4"x3/4" (18x18mm) hardwood or large epoxy fillets

Staggered screws at least 1/2" (50mm) long

Ply bottom of hull

Fig 109. Section through a simple ply skeg.

The profile shape of the skeg/keel can be taken off the upturned hull by making up a hardboard template.

13.1.2 For Medium Sized Dayboats 14'-18' (4.3-5.5m)

In this case, I often use a hollow construction with a wood frame and plywood sides. The hull usually has a hog and the first job is to glue and screw a wood fillet to the outside of the hull which will form the base for the hollow keel or skeg (Figure 110). At roughly 250mm (10") intervals, a vertical wood stiffener is fitted which is capped by an inner bottom fillet. The keel or skeg will often be tapered towards the bottom and if it is easier, the whole skeg can be assembled on the bottom of the hull but can be taken off for finishing on the bench.

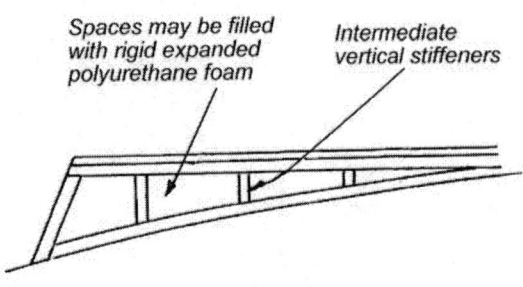

Fig 110. Simple hollow skeg.

The plywood sides can be glued on oversize and trimmed back and the hollow inside may be filled with rigid expanded polyurethane foam (cut from sheet form or poured). In any case, the interior surfaces of the skeg should be epoxy coated or painted. Note that the bottom edge of the ply sides is covered by a hardwood cap (Figure 111).

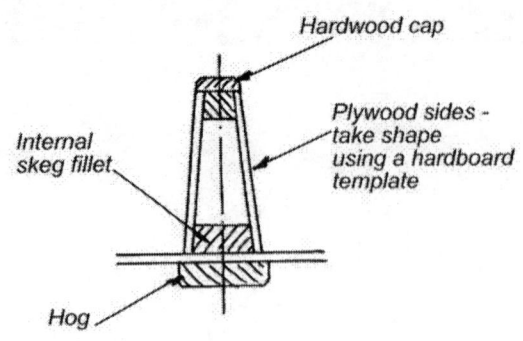

Fig 111. Section though a hollow skeg.

13.1.3 On Larger Dayboats up to 22' (6.7m)

Keels and skegs for larger craft are usually made up in solid wood. Instead of trying to make the shape in one piece I usually glue up in a series of 'lifts' (Figure 112). This works out cheaper and easier than doing the job in one piece.

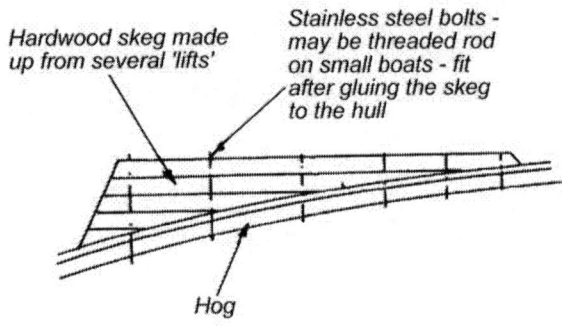

Fig 112. A solid skeg for larger boats.

It is expensive to try and get bolts made up to the required lengths so, it is acceptable on these craft to use rod studding (threaded rod). The bottom lift needs to be pocketed to take the bottom nut and washer. It is also a good idea, especially when using epoxy glue, to glue the lifts together on top of the hull over a sheet of PVC so that it does not glue to the hull. It can then be removed so that it can be planed up on a bench. Once shaped, it can be refitted to the hull and glued in position. At this stage, make sure that it is vertical but do not bolt it into position. This is because tightening the bolts before the glue sets can cause the skeg/keel to move and to lean over to one side. It is much safer to let the glue cure and then to fit the bolts afterwards.

If you do not have drill or auger bitts long enough to make holes right through the skeg and into the hull, then drill through the hull and first lift and then mark the position and drill the holes onto each lift in turn. This can produce rather wild holes but if they are drilled over size and the bolts are inserted in thickened epoxy, this does not usually produce any problems.

13.2 Bilge Keels

Simple bilge keels can be made up from mild steel plate with a flange welded top and bottom as shown in Figure 113. It is less troublesome to make the top flange flat and welded at 90 degrees to the plate bilge keel rather than trying to angle and shape it to follow the curve of the hull bilge. By the time the flange has been welded onto the keel it has usually moved out of position and angle. Take up the shape and different angle of the hull bilge by shaping a hardwood packing piece. If the amount of packing is not too large, then the bilge keel can be fitted and a simple hardboard coffer dam fitted around the flange so that thickened epoxy can be poured into the gap to take up the shape - this is easier done with the boat upside down.

If you are converting your boat to bilge keels, make sure that you arrange for a substantial wood bilge stringer inside the hull to distribute the stresses to the frames etc and use large washer plates under the nuts of the fastening bolts.

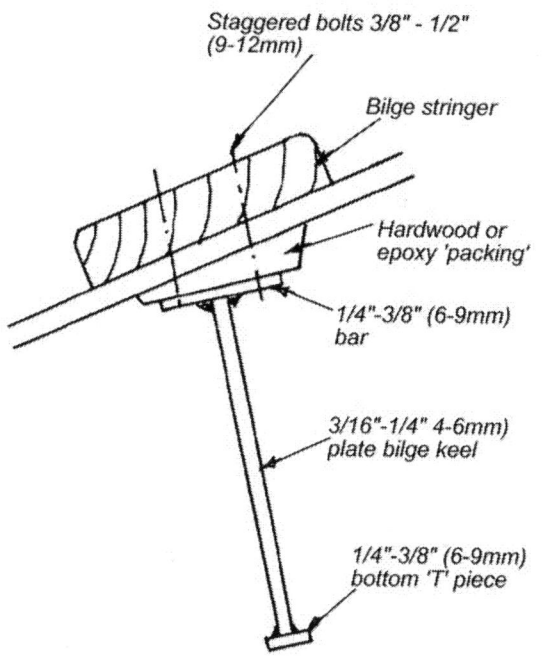

Fig 113. A steel bilge keel.

13.3 Simple Plywood Rudders

The drawings you are working from will give details for the rudder. However, for dinghies, skiffs etc up to about 15' or 16' in length, I have successively used a very simple form of rudder arrangement which looks quite crude but which does the job (Several Phil Bolger/ Dynamite Payson boats use a similar arrangement too) - Figure 114. Rather than having a double cheeked rudder stock with the blade swinging in between, the simple ply stock has both the blade and tiller attached to one side. This can put quite a strain on the pivot bolt which is why this method is only used on small craft and why large stainless steel plate washers are used under both the head and nut of the pivot bolt.

I normally shape the blade so that it has a

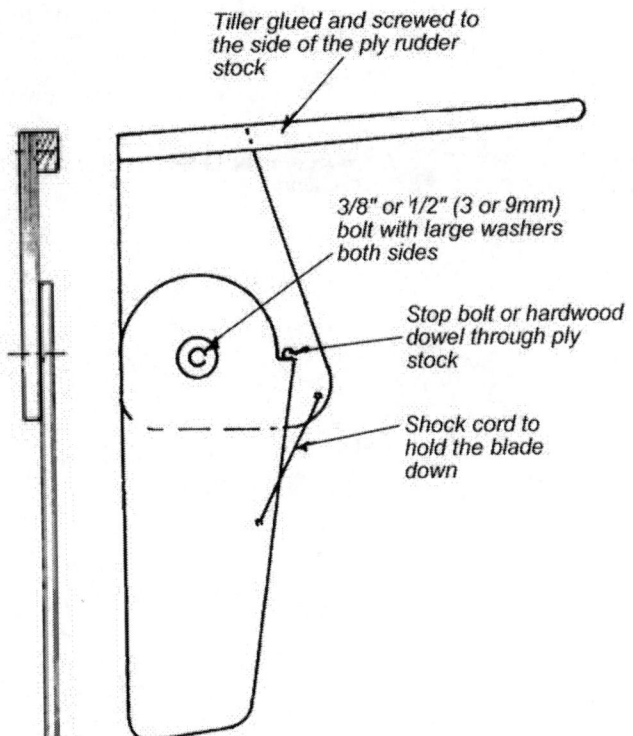

Tiller glued and screwed to the side of the ply rudder stock

3/8" or 1/2" (3 or 9mm) bolt with large washers both sides

Stop bolt or hardwood dowel through ply stock

Shock cord to hold the blade down

Fig 114. A simple rudder with a single ply stock.

knuckle in it, which comes up against a bolt in the stock. This acts as a stop and the blade can then be held down with a piece of shock cord fastened between the blade and the stock. For added sophistication, an uphaul can be arranged from the trailing edge of the blade up to a the tiller. For small dinghies, the stock can be 9 or 12mm (2x6mm) ply and the blade 9mm ply. The largest boat I have used this arrangement on is a 16 footer with an 3/4" (18mm (2x9mm)) stock and 1/2" (12mm) blade.

Rather than having a swing down blade, for long rudders (ie., those with a long cord length - front to back measurement), I have sometimes fitted a 'fence' plate to the bottom edge of the rudder blade (Figure 115). This prevent the 'high pressure' water flow on one side of the blade escaping under the blade to the 'low pressure' side. The high and low

pressures are set up when the rudder is put over and it is the pressure difference between the two sides which gives the boat it's 'turning force' The greater the difference in pressures, the greater the turning force and therefore we want to stop any reduction in this pressure difference. The end 'fence' helps in this and allows the use of a fairly shallow rudder without having to extend the blade deeper by having a swinging portion. This method is not effective enough on narrow rudders and is therefore seen on catboats and the like which have 'barn door' type rudder shapes. I have also used it successfully on skiffs, garvies and dories. If you do not want a swinging rudder blade, it is certainly worth the experiment.

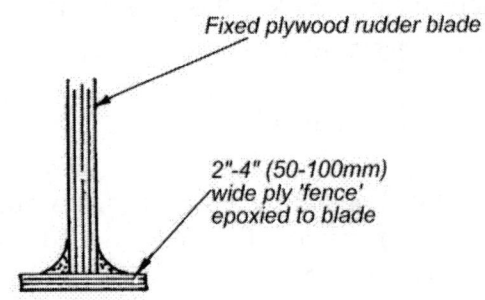

Fixed plywood rudder blade

2"-4" (50-100mm) wide ply 'fence' epoxied to blade

Fig 115. A 'fence' on the bottom of a fixed rudder blade.

13.4 Notes on Simple Joinery

13.4.1 Marking Out & Cutting a Simple Joint

In simple stitch and tape boat construction there is no need for complicated wood joiner work, as modern epoxies can be used to bond pieces of wood together quite successfully using only basic wood joints and sometimes simple butts. As previously mentioned, the use of plywood means that much of the strength of the boat is inherent in the ply skin structure. In traditional boat construction the boat was made out of many small pieces which had to be fitted together carefully and fastened securely. The modern boat on the other hand, is very much a one piece structure with large sheets of wood either in the form of plywood or in the form of a monocoque strip plank or diagonal planked hull. However, some frame structure is required (deck beams, carlins etc) which require some simple wood joins. Many of these joins can be those from the simple halving family of joins (cross halving, tee halving, corner halving and dovetail halving).

One or two points you should note if you are not familiar with simple joiner work are as follows :-

- Do equip yourself with a good square, a sharp pencil and a good tape measure and also use a good sharp backsaw (i.e. tenon saw) and a sharp chisel.
- A large part of the strength of a joint is in the amount of gluing area that it has and therefore the type of joint chosen should depend to a certain extent on this.
- Joints should be planned so that they do not weaken the structure—for instance if you have a stringer crossing a beam and both are of similar depth (moulding), making a simple halving joint and removing half the depth of the beam, may badly effect the strength of the deck structure. Taking less out of the beam and more out of the stringer or using 2 angled halving joints may be better (Figure 116).

We show the sequence for making a good halving join and if you can do this joint, then you can do any of the other joints that are required.

- Firstly mark the sides of the joint using the square across the wood and down each side (Figure 117).
- Note that half the material is removed from each of the pieces of wood therefore either by measuring down and

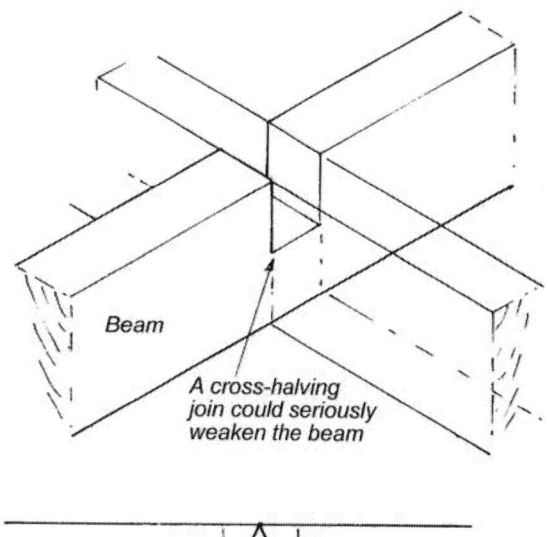

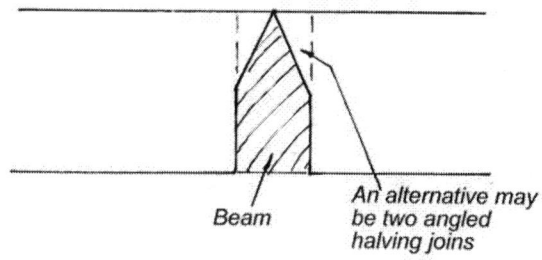

Fig 116. Planning the joins so that the structure is not weakened.

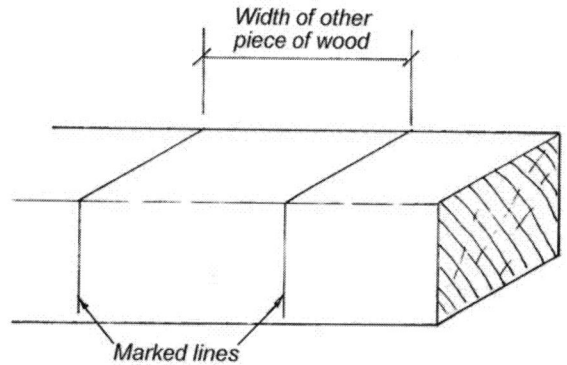

Fig 117. Marking the sides of the join.

drawing across or better still by using a marking gauge (if you can get used to using this tool) mark a line across either side which represents the bottom of the joint (Figure 118).

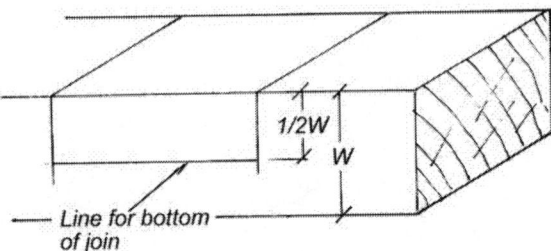

Fig 118. Marking the bottom of a halving join.

- It is a good idea to scribe these lines with a sharp knife cutting through the first few fibres of the wood Figure 119).

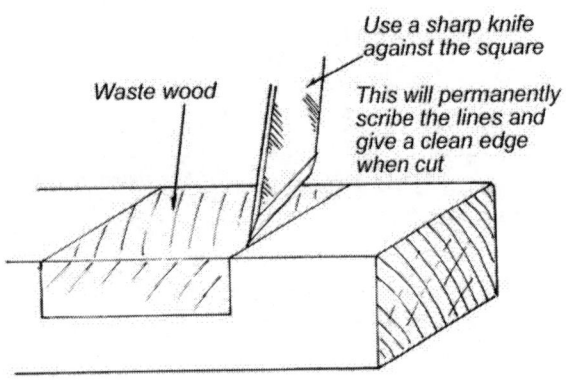

Fig 119. Scribing the join.

- Using your back saw (tenon saw) cut down to the bottom line carefully keeping the saw blade on the waste side of the line as shown. Do this for both lines and then cut two or three lines inside the joint (this will aid you when you come to chisel out the wood. - Figure 120).
- Using the widest chisels possible start from one side of the joint with the

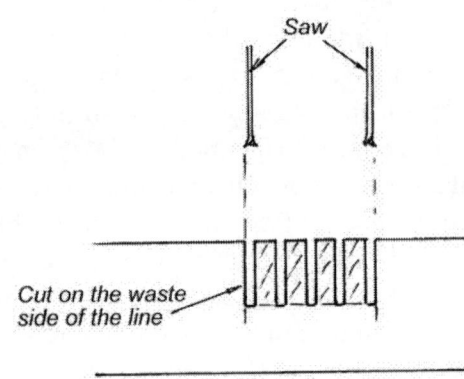

Fig 120. Making the first saw cuts.

chisel 1/8'' from the top and with the chisel angled slightly upwards as shown. Carefully chisel towards the centre of the piece of wood. Come down the side until you are within 1/8'' (3mm) of the bottom.

- Then do the same thing to the other side always working towards the centre of the wood (Figure 121). This will leave you with a small hill in the centre of the wood and you can now clear this out by chiselling horizontally from the top finally going right the way down to the bottom. You will almost certainly find it easier to chisel the wood from one side rather than from the other because of the grain of the wood and therefore you should always do most of your chiselling from the easier side.
- The second piece of wood is marked out in the same way.

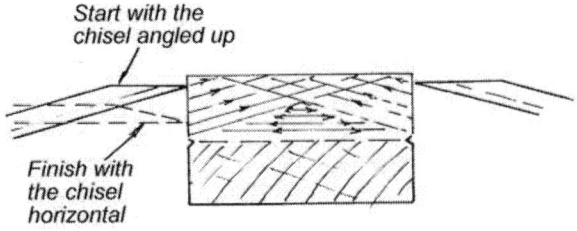

Fig 121. Removing the waste material with a chisel.

94

13.4.2 Other Useful Joints

Cutting right through a piece of wood in order to make a joint does, as we have said, weaken the structure and so an angle halving join is often used especially where beams join with gunwales or carlins (Figure 72 on Page 60). Cutting this join is quite easy and quick—a screw is used through the top of the beam and angled into the inwale or carling.

Quite often now, I find that it is not possible to purchase strips of wood in sufficient length for items such as outwales etc. In this case you need to join two pieces together to make up the full length and for this, I usually use the scarf join (Figure 122).

cutting down through the line keep an eye on the end of the cut closest to you to make sure that you cut vertically down. To cut efficiently and without 'wiggling' the saw as you cut, stand well back so that your arm moves 'in-line' with the line you are cutting.

Alternatively, use a scarf box or jig—this is much the same as a bevel box (used for cutting 45 degree angles) but with the guide cuts at the 1 to 6 or 1 to 8 angle that you want for the scarf join. (Figure 123).

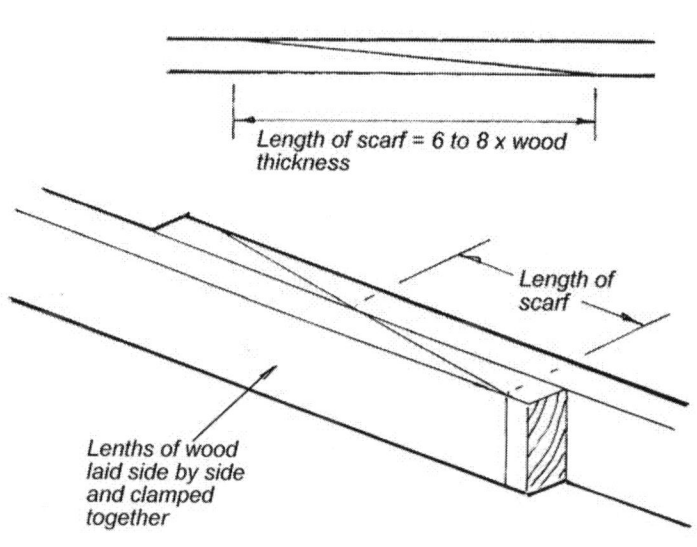

Length of scarf = 6 to 8 x wood thickness

Length of scarf

Lenths of wood laid side by side and clamped together

Fig 122. Setting up to cut a scarf join.

Saw cut to angle of scarf

Fig 123. Above and below, a scarfing box which is worth purchasing or making for yourself if you have several scarf joins to cut.

The scarf is a sloped join (see 5.1.2 for plywood) which has a large gluing area. One way to cut the join is simply to mark the sloped cut line onto each piece and lay them side by side in such a way that both pieces may be cut at the same time. Start the cut at the far end and carefully bring the tenon saw down to onto the marked line—once you are

13.4.3 The Parts of a Simple Stitch & Tape Boat

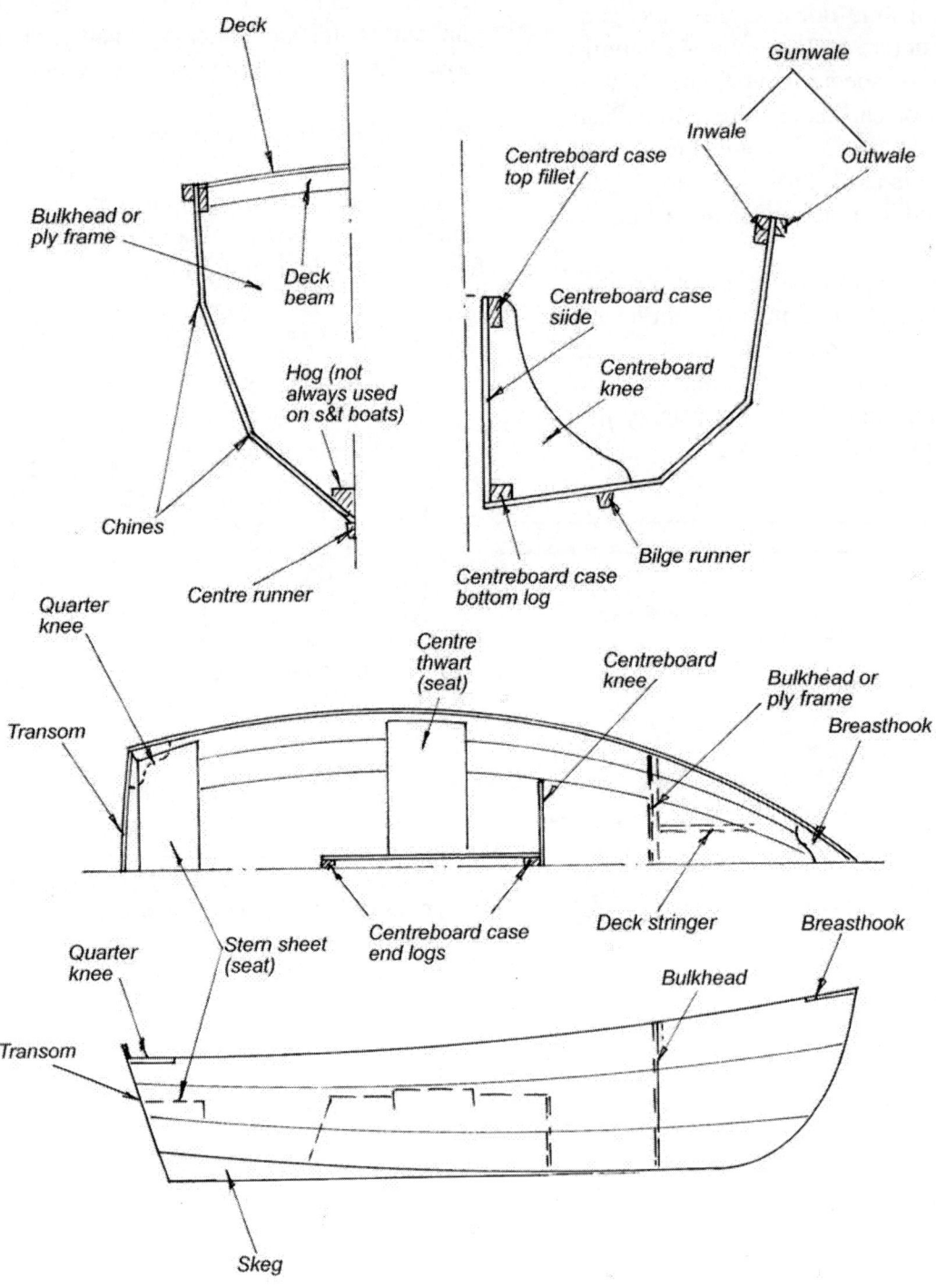

Note—for the names of parts that make up a deck, see 9.6 .